RETHINKING EDUCATION AND DEMOCRACY

A socialist alternative for the twenty-first century

the Hillcole Group
co-ordinated by
Caroline Benn *and*
Clyde Chitty *for*

Pat Ainley
John Clay
Imelda Gardiner
Dave Hill
Ken Jones
Eric Robinson

Shane Blackman
Mike Cole
Rosalyn George
Janet Holland
Glen Rikowski
Julian Wooton

the Tufnell Press

the Tufnell Press,

47 Dalmeny Road,
London, N7 0DY

First published 1997

British Library Cataloguing-in-Publication Data
A catalogue record for this book is
available from the British Library

ISBN 1 872767 45 1

Printed in England by Da Costa Print, London

CN 370
AN 60009

RETHINKING EDUCATION AND DEMOCRACY

the Hillcole Group

The Hillcole Group is a group of Radical Left Educators, formed in 1989 with three aims:

1) To influence policy and decision making on educational matters;

2) To respond rapidly to assaults on the quality of education from the Radical Right;

3) To improve the quality of schooling and of teacher education.

As a writing group, we have been producing a continuous series of publications in pursuit of the above aims. Our earlier books have been critiques of the Radical Right and the way in which their theories and policies have affected schooling, further education and teacher education.

Contents

PRINCIPLES FOR LONG TERM CHANGE

The global context

Most education proposals for the 21st century assume our educational system will remain much the same and that change will come largely in terms of growth: more students, better funding, wider access. By contrast we assume that the 21st century will need an education system very different from that of today, if only because every country will face an explosion in communications, a continuing crisis in employment, growing ecological damage and its own escalating interdependence on the rest of the world.

If education systems are also to assist in protecting democracy in the face of authoritarian governments, whether ruled by military regimes or powerful multinational corporations, education will have to help people to use the new technology to take control of their own lives rather than have it used to control them. For this, information free from manipulation by governments and media empires is essential to enable people to form their own opinions, and needs an education service accountable to the community, to ensure it.

If democracy is to be developed as well as protected, we have to involve growing numbers in decision-making for communities as well as in campaigns to ensure a sharing of useful, fairly paid work for everyone rather than full-time work for some but unemployment or poverty-wages for millions. In industrially advanced countries such sharing would be part of a drive to control an economic system that fuels a runaway gap between over-rich and a growing 'underclass' with an increasingly insecure 'middle'. As the 21st century continues, such drives will increasingly be allied to struggles for social and economic justice in countries where the majority are visibly poor, many without their most basic rights.

Growth can also be expected in the numbers supporting a drive for sustainable economies where society's needs can be met without destruction of the earth's resources that results from over-stimulated consumerism for the purpose of unlimited profit-making. Society will have to see that more time and money and training are spent on renewing and reusing resources to fend off wars over water, wood, fuel and land, to save vanishing species and stop the poisoning of the world by organisations dedicated to profit without concern for the consumers' health, society's welfare or planetary survival.

In short, the 21st century will see our prevailing capitalism being re-questioned by liberal, radical, socialist and ecological movements and ultimately challenged by large sections of world opinion.

The classical socialism of the past was based upon the poor condition of the industrial working class. In future, socialism will be related to everyone, for its aim is not merely to end gross economic inequality; it is also to sustain the world itself, as it gradually becomes apparent that unlimited profit-led development and exploitation of people and non-renewable resources threaten everyone's stability. A world where 358 individual billionaires own as much as 45 per cent of the world's population[1] (as is now the case) is not likely to survive unquestioned.

Behind our long-term education proposals, therefore, is not merely the challenge to capitalism but simple human survival.

Britain's system: a 30 Years' War

Seen within this wider context, Britain's current hierarchical education system with its narrow, elitist preoccupations, seems even more inadequate than it does when viewed within its own national context. The country's economic and social policies have been notoriously short-term and its education plans bedevilled in every field and at every age by elaborations of long-standing historic social divisions from which Britain seems chronically unable to free itself. Once upon a time these divisions were addressed directly, even if remedies proved inadequate; today they are rarely discussed by leading political forces. Indeed, during the 1990s, many proposals (from political parties, think tanks, media columnists) have given positive encouragement to disregard the unequal structures of the system, and have urged new forms of attainment selection and segregated curricula—the very policies that helped sustain divisions in the past.

Today's argument is often misrepresented as a war between loony, liberal radicals and sound, back to basics traditionalists. But this is a false dichotomy because no one person's or group's position conforms to this caricature on either side. More important, a less superficial analysis would show that for the last thirty years there has been a war between a weak social democratic pragmatism, played out in the 1960s and 1970s, and rigid conservative dogmatism, dominating the 1980s and 1990s. Although each made a few positive changes, neither was really successful.

Today a truce is being called on terms far more favourable to conservatism, which started as crude anti-egalitarianism strictly concerned with preserving and increasing social and academic superiority for favoured minorities, but later developed into a grand political strategy of imposing privatisation and capitalist market principles on the education system as a whole.

This was not because 'privatisation' and 'marketisation' ensure better education, but because both reduce public spending on public services and enable savings to be transferred to the private and corporate pockets of the better-off. Consequently, the education system is mimicking the economic: the rich getting richer, while those at the lower half of any education 'league' get poorer, their condition showing itself in deteriorating facilities, increasing alienation and continuing high levels of dropping out. At the same time those in the middle are ever more insecure and doubtful about the quality of the education that they are getting. There is widespread concern as to whether anyone will be able to afford education after 18 in the 21st century or whether our public education service will even exist.

The attack on education is part of the deconstruction of the welfare state (to which a generality of the political leadership now seems to be subscribing) constructing in its place a new contracting post-welfare system, combined with a heavy increase in moralising, which places the blame on those the system is failing. There sometimes seems to be a competition at the top to establish supremacy in tough talking when it comes to the education of the majority, whether it is tracking down 'bad' teachers, chastising 'bad' parents or punishing 'bad' children, along with rooting out 'bad' schools. Everyone wants higher standards of education but can we honestly say that the structure and operation of the education system and the context in which schools operate are as irrelevant as we are now being asked to believe?

Contradictions in the new consensus

Back in 1993 we pointed out that 'in a sort of parody of "permanent revolution", the government is beginning to destroy those elements of its earliest achievements which now appear insufficiently radical' (Hillcole, 1993 c, p. 1). The accelerating pace of the government's educational changes was beginning to undermine its earlier changes deemed insufficiently destructive of some imaginary progressive conspiracy.

Now the hunt for conspirators against 'standards' within the once neutral inspectorate, renamed OFSTED (Office of Standards in Education), finds this mechanism itself producing its own internal debates within an office that is supposed to safeguard the system from fashion, foible and failure, but is increasingly being seen as the mouthpiece of old conservatism (Mortimore, 1997).

Temporarily, conservatism may have the upper hand, but there are deep disagreements within its ranks. On the one hand there are the 'Black Paper' elitists[2], often little Englanders, who believe the British private system leads the world, and state education (except for certain grammar schools) is a distinct second best. For their own children almost all major Conservative politicians and top civil servants, for example, opt out of any experience of the state system used by 93 per cent of the nation.

For some in this group this is part of their commitment to Britain as a low-wage economy, competing successfully with the 'third world', workers needing only to learn how to assemble components for multinational factories, or run the service sector increasingly required to provide for the better-off. The generality of the population does not need extensive, expensive schooling; they need education for service, obedience, basic skills and learning in socio-economic and social matters that inculcates 'the right kind' of thinking. As they did in the first industrial revolution.

There is another kind of conservative, including several industrial gurus and business people, unimpressed by attainment selection, and a few large multinationals, supportive of comprehensive schools. And although the Confederation of British Industry (CBI) may be committed to a right-wing economic strategy and a capitalist future for the world, it too remains largely aloof from nostalgia for some imagined high quality past and at least attempts to be robustly enterprising. It has invested its hopes in a 'cultural revolution' of sorts (*Towards a Skills Revolution*, 1989) by backing a programme that would encourage more individual self development and lifetime learning, focusing on a multi-skilled future for as many as possible rather than on a return to the selective past for some. This kind of conservative, to be found in all political parties, has a vested interest in the European Union and the imagined discipline of co-operative capitalism that until recently has produced highly skilled workers and higher rates of employment in many European countries.

The proposals of this camp are, however, marked by a conspicuous fault line between aspiration and the realities of what British business and industry, left to their own short-term priorities, have ever been able to deliver. Universal training policy sits uncomfortably alongside the unlikely prospect of UK employers being able to incorporate the unemployed at any level in any numbers, young or old, with or without qualifications. By itself British industry, which even resists paying a tiny levy for training, cannot achieve modernisation without putting a great deal more of its own investment into education and training; and it might be short-sighted to continue pretending it can.

Nor are the CBI's own publications optimistic. On training they leave a reader worried about the retention of the largely unsuccessful Training and Enterprise Councils (TECs), Local Enterprise Councils (LECs) in Scotland), which administer training and enterprise programmes, with their 'uneven quality' and great 'disparity' in approach, as well as the market's failure to use school leavers, whatever their qualifications (CBI, 1994, p. 20). CBI optimism about the new people-centredness of industry is belied by its admission that there is indeed a 'two-tier workforce' (CBI, 1994, p. 24). The highly skilled might be secure but the rest are to be used and then discarded.

Workers of the 1990s know that the much-trumpeted 'flexibility' of the 1980s has turned out to be a euphemism for disposability in the 1990s. Conservatism, as we approach the new millennium, has little to offer other than its own internal bickering between a 'nationalist' and 'European' version of capitalism, neither providing a long-term workable alternative in either education or the economy.

New Labour: How new a policy?

Labour's decisive win in the general election of 1997 provides a wonderful opportunity for a fresh start, despite the fact that Labour policy pronouncements maintain a detachment from commitment in many of the most debated areas of education, while suggesting that radical change is possible. Instead, they offer a soothing scenario as in the economy at large: socio-economic change of the degree and kind required to end polarisation and economic insecurity by means that are wholly 'benign' and involve no real change or fundamental challenge to economic policy or social system. The view seems to be that, because a change is required, it will occur even in the present unchallenged economic system; and that educational change with greater equality, fairer distribution of resources and mass improvement will occur even in the present inequitable education system—if ministers insist on it.

Promising higher standards by exhorting practitioners but refusing to examine the system in which they practise, avoids the issue that it is the structure of the education system overall which divides Britain. In particular, it demotivates many students from disadvantaged groups, and will continue to lead to polarisation. Like all who seek to address the quality of education without addressing the quality of social or economic life as a whole, Labour's fundamental promises—concerning universal access and a rapid rise in levels of attainment—could be hard to achieve without a much wider social focus than Labour has envisaged to date.

Of course there can be improvements and a Labour Government will deliver some. But Labour begins with some gigantic concessions to existing discontent: Grant Maintained (GM) schools stay, albeit in new legal guise; private education is untouched and still enjoys substantial state subsidies, despite the end of the Assisted Places scheme[3]; the unimpressive TECs and LECs retain their huge budgets outside the education system and outside locally elected accountability rather than using these funds to support an extension of education and training programmes run by public colleges in co-operation with democratically accountable bodies. Overall, proposals for the regeneration of local democracy, much touted, are as yet unformed outside promises for devolution for Scotland and Wales and a London mayor.

After all this time there is even ambiguity about ending the '11-plus' process still kept in being by a significant number of grammar schools in England, as well as a lack of clarity about reforming admissions systems, and little prospect of ending 'league table' divisiveness (since 'value added' proposals do nothing to end polarisation even if they do add an extra dimension to individual school judgements). The biggest concession is to the market itself, putting Labour's education programme inadvertently in danger of becoming an alternative conservative policy, not an alternative policy that will tackle what the *Times Educational Supplement* (TES) and others have repeatedly called the hierarchy of status into which all schools and colleges are now being forced. Policy fails to confront the alarming prospect of a future bedevilled by continued social and economic polarisation, which will be inevitable unless amended by political action.

There is a also a dearth of proposals to deal with inequality. Some policies seem likely to increase it: like specialising comprehensives free to select on 'aptitude' and discouragement for new forms of unstreamed teaching (with no apparent knowledge of their potential or of the limited use today of old forms); or the pitfalls of subject streaming or segregated post-14 pathways. The continued imposition of a much-disputed 'National'

Curriculum framework, with its 'streaming' of teachers as well as dictating how and what they should teach, will be examined eventually, but what of meanwhile?

There are no firm proposals yet to integrate academic and vocational education, to give everyone wider curriculum choice, leaving Dearing's anaemic changes to stem the tide of renewed pressure from conservatives for internal 'tracking' of schools. Above all, there has been widespread dismay at the failure to give positive encouragement and support to the principle of comprehensive education itself. Ironically, just when it has attained a commanding lead in public opinion.[4] No wonder there is some suspicion that Labour leaders and advisers (as distinct from the Labour Party) are seeking to bury the comprehensive idea and that its 'modernising' policy will lead to the reintroduction of the grammar/ secondary modern division inside schools themselves.

What policy proposals are made raise few objections because they reinforce the *status quo* in terms of the basic operation of the system, while also insisting on yet more activities schools, teachers and parents must undertake whether they like it or not. Many are coming from an increasingly contracting inner circle of 'experts' who 'unveil' them from on high, risking consequent failure by the learning community to claim that 'ownership' so essential to getting ideas acted upon within institutions.

Outside the compulsory sector there is still some lack of clarity about the proposals for pre-5 education, particularly over the way education will be combined with day-care provision; and fewer plans of substance for the rational and cost-effective reorganisation of 16-19 education in 1997 than were put forward in Labour's publications in the 1970s and 1980s.[5] As for post-18 policy, the Labour Party is content to farm out the future to the ubiquitous Dearing: giving his team *carte blanche* to recommend future higher education policy separate from policy for the majority of post-18 students' education in further education, as well as to concentrate on solutions dominated by the market. In the event the government decided even before Dearing reported that for university students, grants and loans would be replaced by fees and loans. Despite remission of fees, the loan debt for the poorest would be higher than for those whose families could afford to contribute.

Making the most of democratic change

But since Labour's 1997 victory there has been a sea-change in society's hopes for itself and thus a chance for alternatives to be debated. So, let us assume the best: that there will be some questioning of the leading role of the market as the sole arbiter of education policy, and even some attempt to resurrect the role of local and regional government; that there will be key legislative changes to reorient the system in the direction of non-selective education from 5 to 19; that there will be some dismantling of self-perpetuating oligarchies in schools and colleges, some audit of equality among social groups; and even some additional funding beyond that already designated. Can these measures succeed if they remain minimal in scope or inadequately funded; can they engage parents and teachers and lecturers and students and communities if they are a continuation of top-down imposition from the central government, unrelated to renewed popular activity at ground level?

And how far could such a policy avoid a return to the old post-war social democratic consensus, a consensus that collapsed precisely because it was so inadequate?

For example, despite decades and millions spent on equal opportunity measures, no real dent has ever been made in the monopoly of educational chances by the wealthy, the educationally knowledgeable and the traditional upper-middle classes. Though particular groups, like middle-class women and some upwardly-mobile Asian, black, and other minority ethnic groups, have made progress, the working class as a whole (which, however defined, is still a substantial proportion of society, e.g., in the latest census 50 per cent of all men[6]) has not made significant progress. Large swathes of outer and inner city areas have regressed significantly, and over-pressed educators' own work on equal opportunities has lapsed in many areas, especially inside schools and colleges (Benn and Chitty, 1996).

The intractable inequalities of a class system that is encouraged in its divisions by the national education structure are a brake upon educational improvement in many parts of Britain, as is recognised elsewhere in the world. Not without interest, President Clinton's main political advisor, explaining why Clinton was concentrating on a whole 'package of education reforms', stressed it was a change which 'has to happen so we can make sure we are not turning into an old fashioned European class system, where the children of people at the bottom stay at the bottom'.[7]

Both social democratic consensus and all forms of conservatism shared the same fault: a political approach that was inadequate, where 'we' gave 'them' opportunities processed from the top down rather than greater empowerment of parents, teachers, students of all ages and all sorts of communities, to make their own way. Education was inherently paternalistic under the social democratic model, and inherently dictatorial under the conservative. Neither system encouraged teachers or learners or institutions enough or gave them the wherewithal to act for themselves in many areas of education; neither promoted innovation or enthusiasm for the development of learning within the community to engage both children and adults in large numbers.

Except in the most exceptional of experiments, neither widened definitions of intelligence and achievement in learning within the education system, or encouraged more than a few new forms of assessment, so that the full range of intelligences could be tapped and recorded in both children and adults. And neither devised means to measure progress that did other than reinforce the old hierarchies of 'excellence' in terms of narrow 'academic' success. Today this means that selection is creeping back and infecting area after area of education, often using 'choice', 'diversity', 'standards' and 'specialisation' as camouflage. All good words that are now tainted.

Lack of popular support

In recent decades equity and equality have been overridden by the market. The education system—like the health care system and the social system—drifts towards increasing polarisation. Some groups with better education, topping league tables, living in affluent areas or with advantaged admissions systems, are able to benefit by the many forms of selection or by public spending which goes to them disproportionately. On the other side of the line, others are often in decaying inner cities and neglected housing estates or areas abandoned to dereliction, enduring ever worsening conditions, attention and prospects, particularly for employment. The policy approach of conservatism is that the context of schooling is irrelevant, and the same for structure. It is only standards that matter. Yet the world over it is known that standards are conditioned by context and depend on structure, just as much as upon good teaching.

Students and pupils of all ages react to experiences that arise from poor context and unfair structure by truanting, addiction and self-destructive behaviour, or much the most common: indifference and the desire to escape education as quickly as possible. And no wonder. In a market system a formalised, extended system of league tables for individuals and institutions during the whole length of compulsory education now teaches the 'bottom' half of the population that they are 'failures' which is far more discouraging than the old '11-plus' because it is continual, not just once for all.

It is curious that conservatism's prescriptions should still be so strong, for, as we wrote earlier (Hillcole, 1993 c, p. 4): 'the new right has negligible supports within education'. Many political leaders seem oblivious of the most fundamental defect embedded in so much educational change in the last fifteen years: it never arose from popular demand. The issues addressed may have been popular, like more choice and better information, but the policies devised to deliver them were not.

Popular opinion may want higher standards, better funding, helpful assessment, and an equalisation of opportunities as well as an extension of learning. But no majority of parental or teacher or lecturer or local authority or civil service opinion ever supported projects like the National Curriculum (in the form introduced by Baker and his colleagues), perpetual mass testing in the form being introduced, or the 'league table' version of comparative information—not to mention vouchers, opting out, privatisation, reduction of local democratic accountability, and the virtual abandonment of planning.

For these changes, the Conservative Government had to rely for eighteen years on two pillars alone: the support of the media and the powers of Westminster office, using a strategy of never-ending (and often hastily conceived) legislative changes. The pressure was reinforced through financial cuts and moves to control the system in the interests of certain sections of society over others. To do this (against the interests of so many) has been an exhausting business and any new government seeking to adopt the same strategy will find this out. It is exhausting in the wider world as well. Cuts in fairly won and widely supported improvements continue to generate resentment whether taking place in public services, firms' 'restructuring', the EU disciplining of national economies to satisfy the banks, or the world bank disciplining the developing world to accept poor wages and poorer conditions—all required for the maximum functioning of capitalism.

Resistance

Of course there is resistance, and it contributed to the anti-Conservative electoral victory in 1997. When we predicted (Hillcole, 1993 c, p. 2) that the 'current and planned-for changes will bring about failure and provoke opposition to an extent that will imperil the whole Conservative project in education', we little realised the extent to which teachers and parents, for example, in that year and the next, bypassing an equivocating political opposition, would demonstrate their refusal to continue with the extremes of destructive testing and imposed curriculum regimes. Resistance was even stronger in Scotland, where it still continues.

To cut opposition short at that time, carelessly introduced proposals were equally hastily modified, but inevitably—with no alternative proposals being forwarded—the changes that took their place were only a little less destructive, spilling out of far-right think tanks, those tiny and interlocked groups so influential in the years of Conservative Government. Such changes as: a return to grammar schools for every area; a wasteful oversupply of school places in order to retain 'choice' for a minority; and mass testing running riot from infant years onwards—with 'results' used, as feared, not to assist learning and teaching for everyone but to rank individuals and institutions (boosting some but shaming and blaming others).

The pressure for a continuation of comprehensive education, so long monopolised by the compulsory years, is now moving on to the years before 5 and after 16. This has spawned utterly unworkable and costly voucher systems (and 'credit' systems in training) poised to subsidise private provision in every area of education and training, but actually preventing pre-5 expansion in both state and voluntary sectors and hardly making a dent on the training of the young unemployed. Nursery vouchers are going but has the old voucher idea gone for good?

In the years 14 to 19 we have a proposed consolidation of outdated tripartite education embedded in the proposed post-16 curriculum (now being retroactively forced on the years 14 to 16) from the ever-obedient Ron Dearing, again against the recommendations of almost all national bodies which have submitted plans for the far future, where a wide common core and progressive integration of vocational and academic education are what have been identified as needed.[8] In view of this, suggestions in the summer of 1997 that the government might rethink the curriculum and assessment for 16-19 were welcomed.

Even the growth of numbers going on to higher education since 1990 has been used to signal an end to the entitlement to free higher education, while competition is ensuring resource-cutting and closures in further and higher education colleges, not to mention renewed apprehension about 'training' schemes that substitute conditional workfare for the benefits which social insurance payments were supposed to have guaranteed. Meanwhile, adults struggle to secure 'life-long' opportunities in the face of a much reduced offering in the 'independent', business-led colleges, as well as against vested higher education interests seeking to retain and extend post-18 selection.

Alternatives

The lesson is that conservative education policy, to borrow an old phrase, isn't working. Its many and manifest failings have evoked, since 1990, a surge of alternative thinking, from a variety of political quarters. All perceive that emphasis on the market, at the core of conservative policy in education, accentuates inequalities, and a growth in 'distressed areas' in education. Unfortunately, a change in government has yet to produce any definite alternative itself in any overall sense—other than promises of better 'management' of the existing setup along with exhortation to serve the many, not the few. All this is very welcome, but is it enough?

The National Commission on Education (1993) at least recognised the disabling divisions of the British education system which led to minority success and majority frustration. It particularly noted the failure for decades of the working class to increase its share of education at higher levels. It suggested useful short-term changes like bringing vocational and academic education closer and moving away from a subject centred curriculum in schooling. But its prescriptions are entirely limited by economic perspectives which endorse the necessities of international competition on a free market basis; its proposals are conceived in 'top down' terms and reflect the concerns of dominant social groups. Its model of change is bureaucratic and, having no experience of the cultures of the majority, leaves little space for local or popular initiatives which would pave the way to mass participation in education.

In particular, it does nothing to deal with possibly the single most urgent problem education has suffered over the last few decades: the draining away of democratic accountability in all its constituent parts. In this respect, some of the Commission's proposals are positively dangerous: that the undemocratic TEC and LEC oligarchies should take over from elected local authorities.

The Commission for Social Justice in 1994 was another body offering solutions, borrowing many progressive ideas from the National Commission. These two in turn seemed for a while to have influenced Labour Party thinking, though Labour's *Opening Doors to a Learning Society* (1994) was more ambitious than either. In the latter's pronouncements there were some encouraging signs: reorienting expenditure towards the earlier years, backing for individualised learning (in and out of school contexts), the linking of study and work, ending selection. They stressed community and showed some realisation that a framework of collective social provision was necessary. But how much of this document now survives?

Are the existing alternatives adequate?

Welcome though it was to find that several policy documents from the Institute of Public Policy Research (IPPR, 1990 and 1993) called for such changes as the scrapping of A level, upgraded and integrated vocational education and training, the establishment of universal nursery education, most (even if enacted) would hardly qualify as radical, since comparable 'western' societies have already introduced almost all of them. They are plans for catching up, not going forward. Even the hardly radical Clinton administration's plans for the USA include the extension of comprehensive education beyond secondary school—up to two years of higher education for everyone, making 14 years of education up to the age of 20. Similar changes are taking place in other countries.

Nor are qualifications really the Big Idea they started out to be in the early 1990s. The new hierarchy of qualifications being imposed on learners at work and in education threatens to turn the qualified society into the certified society—a new system of divide and rule. It is employer oriented, not learner oriented; urged on us for the health of a multinational capitalist world market rather than the interests of our own neighbourhoods or our own wider social or personal development. There is lip service about communities but little that fosters any collective advance.

The one-sided approach is individualist throughout, ironically limiting many individuals' development, for the chance of 'getting on' still narrows dramatically within the British educational system, as it did in days past. By the time even the end of secondary education is reached, the majority have already fallen at the hurdles the system imposes. More survive now than ten years ago but the point is: it is still a system of hurdles—not a system of doors that can be opened one by one, as the learners themselves decide to open them. As one eminent educationalist has often been heard to joke, 'No matter how far you go in English education, they'll fail you in the end'.

All too often education systems, including our own, still use failure to define themselves—rather than exploring ways of ensuring success. Until this is changed, major improvements will be difficult, if not impossible. This is why we believe that changing the system in a new direction requires a much larger change in our own culture than is presently envisaged.

A new culture of education means a new social culture and a new economy

We believe society is ready to start moving in a new direction and abandon two decades of rightwards policy exploration that now leaves no future except ever more unworkable and unpopular possibilities. At the same time we believe that neither a market-led modernisation of society on the one hand, nor, on the other, the old social democratic, corporatist order, which the market displaced, can meet the needs of a 21st century society or the individuals within it. We cannot rely on 'state solutions' alone; even if they are supportive. The only alternative is an education system that can offer the democratic reconstruction and cultural regeneration of society that is daily becoming more necessary if we are to ensure adequate social provision while also modernising the economy. Our objectives are very long term but it is long term change that is required.

Despite our misgivings, we do not wish to undervalue the salutary effects that will come from ending nearly 20 years of official conservatism—where the popular perception is one of education being cut in quantity and quality while the democratic perception is of education being subject to ever more unaccountable central direction. This central direction has been accompanied by a new breed of 'inspectors' and 'quangocrats' poised to crack the whip on all who do not do it the way conservative's think-tankers have prescribed, which largely works out to the benefit of the social and economic groups in society who have already received the most benefit.

New hope will be unleashed but education is unlikely to do more than inch ahead, particularly in the long run, until the culture of education itself has been reoriented in a new direction. This is unlikely to happen if the driving force for change is limited to the narrow need for British industry to compete ever more fiercely in an ever more stridently market-driven world, overseen by media moguls who can 'buy' the right to enforce their views on as many as they can pay to reach. Or where the choice is between an inward-looking nationalism or world-bank internationalism, patrolled by the American military, with a more or less permanent division of 'advanced capitalism' from the rest of the world, and full protection for multinational corporations' operations regardless of the consequences. Without encouragement for wider thought and education about alternative economic and social systems for the world, 'free' and unrestrained capitalist development will proceed by its own laws and very possibly result in unacceptable levels of destructive change.

There may be occasional pleas for more concern for the disadvantaged or some endangered species, spurred by compassion or the inability of even the very rich to escape the effects of diminishing nature and pollution. But an increase in ozone protection is a limited objective, not the social or economic redistribution of wealth and power in the world that would be necessary to really challenge a whole range of destructive practices. We need to turn development around towards co-operative, redistributive, mutually agreed laws related to sustainable development, devised by a representative range of human beings acting in their several societies on criteria that put the survival of the human race and its planet before the iron law of profit. This is a struggle that has to be consciously 'socialist'—in the sense that it is about society itself—in order to succeed.

Section II

What are the conditions of a successful alternative?

An alternative education policy means moving in the direction of an alternative society. It cannot be superimposed on a society that operates through support for undisciplined market capitalism and multinational development as it presently exists.

Conservative policy has shown the limits of this approach in the United Kingdom and in this sense has done us a favour. The conservative position has taken economic policy to the point where it has to end, showing clearly that its aim is to control thinking by closing off consideration of most alternative social or economic systems. In education it is the same, with the argument over OFSTED's policing role only one example. Education is there to express one view—conservatism's own; and one culture—Old England's. This is achieved through one right curriculum; one right way of teaching—even of learning to read; one right way of grouping pupils for learning; one right policy for doing homework; one right way of assessment and preparing learning materials; one right way of thinking about economic systems. All of this leads to one right way of managing the economy under the only system possible for world market capitalism.

Although conservatives claim diversity and freedom as goals, and push 'deregulation' for profit makers, they are always forced to challenge real diversity and real freedoms when the showdown comes with those who disagree with their model for society or for the education system serving it. They have regulated the whole meaning of educational 'reform' to accord with the interests of those who agree with their own thinking. This is why changes underwrite the system and promote the present economic and social system as the only choice. Its superficial workings can be adjusted but not its fundamental basis.

Its fundamental basis, as we have seen throughout this century, despite popular and revolutionary challenges to the existing order, is marked by one notable characteristic that cannot be changed: polarisation. Time was when such extremes were a matter for regret but today we have a polarised society both within and between nations—often with no apologies. It is the 'iron law of capitalism' to have a system that works in favour of those who are favoured by actively working against those who are not.

We do not accept this and we do not believe that in the long run the majority of people will be willing to accept it.

Renewed commitment to democratic organisation and accountability

Of the several changes required, the first is democratic accountability— even though our society is presumed in most existing education policy-making, party-political or extra-parliamentary, to be fully free and democratic. Parliament is unquestioned as highly effective (give or take some changes in its rules of election), while the European Union is largely accepted in its present formulation of Commission-led decision-making, give or take a degree or two of national veto. The world's development is also settled, we are told for 'the rest of history', gurus tell us, we will be subject to a full-blown capitalist market system.

In Britain there may be proposals for different voting systems, such as proportional representation, to end 'adversarial party politics' (IPPR, 1993, p. 21) or different views about how to relate to Europe (Little Englander Capitalism vs Corporate European Capitalism); or different proposals for streamlined procedures, such as fewer parliamentary seats or more appointed or elected peers, or a Royal Family living in two or three palaces rather than two dozen; and internationally, new ways to organise the military action of the United Nations through better NATO oversight. But there is no real discussion of alternative social or economic systems for society.

This makes it hard to put forward a new vision for education in the 21st century, to recoup the loss of credibility education is suffering, especially as party political infighting rages round practices which to the naked eye seem entirely similar, and everyone experiences a continuing loss of democratic accountability throughout the system. There is little policy in sight as yet for restoring such accountability in new and radical ways. What there is leads us to expect elaborate constructs for consensual models, very much like the failed consensus models of the past.

Even the most forward looking of the papers (IPPR, 1993) recommends only that 'citizens' construct a 'vision together with government' where 'interest groups' will 'participate' in policy making, thus conjuring up a perpetual Great Debate that leaves the direction of education to an alliance of the knowledgeable and politically vetted, while most education workers and the mass of education's participants are mere spectators to the process. Yet time was even in Britain when it was assumed it might be possible for everyone involved in education—teachers, learners, education workers of every kind, as well as those elected to bodies by virtue of a democratic vote—to have a collective say in the way education should work, as a way of encouraging mass participation in the education system.

To achieve that mass participation, we have to be able to question our system fundamentally. For example, if administration is too centralised and local authorities too weak, what powers and duties should regional or local governments have in education? Or if choice is just a mirage, as so many say, what rights should individuals or groups or communities be able to ask for with regard to education at all stages? And what should institutions like schools or colleges individually or collectively be able to do? What new 'institutions' are needed? And how differently might learning develop in future in ways more accessible to people? There is little thinking of this kind—and most would say there cannot be, since funding is finite. This will always be so, but the way the funds are apportioned is infinite. It is this that should be open to discussion.

Life-long education is not just more evening classes

There may be some discussion, for example, of the way money in secondary spending might be shifted towards the primary or pre-school years, but little willingness to tackle the massively disproportionate and regressive funding of post-18 education in the UK and hardly any thought about the urgent need to restructure the whole of this system in time for genuine 'life-long' education to make the headway it will require to sustain society in the 21st century.

For many, life-long education is still merely a question of more evening classes for the elderly, the unemployed or for those with hobbies. Few understand that the growing movement behind life-long learning is a commitment to making it possible for anyone, any time, anywhere to take up education of any kind, on their own or their community's behalf. This is a very different and far more revolutionary concept.

It is also a concept competing for funds with other traditional claims on funds. Will there be, for example, any furthering of the freedom/privilege debate, to test the current position that private education is simply an issue of freedom but not an issue of privilege, especially when so many millions from the taxpayers are still supporting private education rather than being put to meet majority need in the public education service? Time was when progressives committed themselves to dealing with diversion of public funds through 'charity' status or state payment of fees for army officers' and civil servants' children, using the same arguments the government applied in support of its 1997 legislation to end Assisted Places.[9]

The same principle also needs debating in relation to the state use of many private training firms and private colleges in preference to the funding of publicly supported colleges and their courses. As well as to the continued underwriting of the Oxbridge colleges, whose accountability to the tax community which so richly supports them, is even more remote and protected from democratic examination in terms of their place and influence in the education system and in research.

With the coming of life-long education, we need a new look at institutions as well as new definitions of standards, freedom, choice, discipline and diversity—all concepts which have been hijacked to reduce variety, increase centralised control and allow many privileges to remain largely unexamined.

New forms of democratic control and organisation

In state supported education resources have been progressively restricted, with institutions given illusory 'powers to police dwindling funding' in the name of local institutional control. Meanwhile, out of everyone's control, resources overall are increasingly inequitably distributed, barely any longer accountable to locally or regionally elected members of the community, and often in the hands of those appointed to quangos by patronage and party machines. Many state-funded 'independent' schools and colleges today (and increasingly 'specialising' institutions) have little democratic relationship or obligation to their communities. They exist to promote their own self-interest. No community can of itself insist that as recipients of public funding, they take part in democratic educational development locally, regionally and nationally. This defect is central.

A new policy has to confront these anti-democratic developments, as well as unfair educational laws, in order to effect the far-reaching change in the culture of education that is required to head us towards a system that fosters genuine, self-directed, self-disciplined, socially critical and individually responsible learning which everyone can access. For this to occur, we will have to move beyond both the old corporate approach and today's fashionable 'command classroom'.

Our objective is a widespread participatory democracy and a renewal of planning for comprehensive opportunity in all parts of the education system. We intend our proposals to contribute to a society where people will be knowledgeable, skilled, critical, and confident—rather than passive, insecure, indifferent victims of economic necessity, which is what a market-led world will always produce for a large proportion of the population. We want to see people as agents of change rather than as mere objects of economic necessity.

That is why we try to look at the future differently—as a prospect which can be shaped by human action, and is not forever fixed by an inhuman 'market' which dictates ironclad terms. We know in our own history that improvements for the majority which finally did take place after the mass poverty of the industrial revolution, did not come from conservatism and the market. These improvements came from the voluntary activity of thousands and the social and political organisation of the common population, including the dispossessed and those discriminated against. They found at times a democratic majority who supported them, including the majority of the labour movement, and took political and social action. Today many are helping the 'third world's' disadvantaged to organise in precisely the same way. This is a fundamental necessity for any alternative system.

Universalise the capacity for critical enquiry

The second requirement is a renewed drive to develop in all citizens, from the beginning of life to the end, the capacity for critical enquiry.

For proposing an alternative in education must begin with acknowledging that few are educated to think in terms of alternatives at any level, not just to the way education is conducted but to the way society is run or even to the new areas where knowledge and expertise can be legitimately developed. Most alternatives to education or to society as both are now run, are ruled out of bounds. That is the central problem.

Recent amendments to the 'National' Curriculum in secondary schools, particularly at Key Stage Four, have meant that much study of society itself, and of history, both areas in which students of all ages are often interested, has been squeezed out of the timetable. In further education, the space that once permitted critical thinking for generations of working people, general education, has been removed; in initial teacher education disciplines like philosophy, psychology and sociology have been progressively eliminated, reduced or changed in nature, while funding pours into a proliferation of 'business studies' and vocational qualifications (some first rate but many of poor quality).

Britain already has twice as many business education courses as any other comparable country. What it does not have is twice as good a record in economic growth. Nor does it have an equally large number of alternative studies that relate directly to the provision of public services, environmental protection, peace promotion or poverty reduction at home or world wide. These again are areas of learning that command widespread interest in the population but which rarely appear as legitimate 'subjects' in the official knowledge of school or college. Why does it not pay to give qualifications or degrees in so many of the fields that society needs—or allow them to enter the school curriculum?

There is very little critical examination by any of the political parties of genuine alternative policy, and this is a matter of common enough comment. On a wider scale, there has been little open-minded assessment of the socialist experiments in Eastern European countries before they degenerated into state capitalism and even further into 'market' capitalism, other than to assume every aspect of their systems, including their education, failed; and to continue to hunt for models in tightly controlled or downright dictatorial regimes emulating 'western' economies. Yet much of the education in these high-growth areas is problematic and much of that under old communism was highly effective.

Have we nothing to learn from old communism's system, despite its democratic failure, or indeed from the failure of social democracy to bring about the changes it claimed it could; or from countries like Cuba which despite its desperate economic situation (exacerbated by the American boycott) and stale state bureaucracy, has nevertheless consistently improved its people's health and education to levels even many advanced and 'western' nations have yet to reach? Can we not learn from societies, and cultures, in the world that proceed quite differently from our own, some by working 'with' rather than against nature? Or from alternative experiments within our own cultures, which rarely get promoted or discussed other than as curiosities?

Narrowing of thinking sometimes seems like the aim of our system, not some inadvertent result. Encouragement to think widely in terms of technological development that will contribute to the market in computers and information technology—that is permissible. But not changing the nature of society itself. In *Learning to Succeed* (NCE 1993) people are encouraged to 'think for themselves' but it is thinking tightly within a capitalist framework, where employers' needs still dominate, and the thinking to be done revolves around better understanding of the profit-making work undertaken by employers in a world where 'wealth creation' is no longer an activity of those who work, as it was at the start of the 20th century, but rather of the owners of capital.

Education is where thinking about alternatives starts

We would not wish to suggest that there is no thinking going on about the future and the way society could be improved, only that the frame in which it is constrained is one of the narrowest that history has ever known. We would not wish to imply no thought goes into redressing the way nature is being mutilated or that a few are not seriously debating alternatives to a global market economy which is dominated by multinationals encroaching upon life, learning, culture and the environment; only that these efforts are not widely disseminated in mainstream education. Learning about them has to take place 'in our own time' for it is thinking not officially sanctioned in a market world, or in the UK blessed by our 'National' Curriculum and dominated by business degrees. Yet it is largely within the educational process that productive changes in thought have to come, making that leap from analysis to activity.

We know groups living in dictatorships are debating alternatives even while we ignore their lack of freedoms or forward arms to their leaders. In other countries it is pseudo-dictatorships, oligarchies and absolute monarchies that are left to oppress; and our media and political leaderships usually react to them not on principle but according to commercial interest. When commercial rivalry leads to conflict (as in the Falklands/Malvinas or the Gulf) good citizens will be whipped into a frenzy of hate and told to defend 'our way of life' against an enemy practising by exactly the same economic rules. Capitalist competition has always led from trade wars to real wars. How many times do we have to re-learn this lesson?

How many times do we to learn the lesson that global capitalism sometimes requires us to co-operate with, or remain powerless before, cartels and monopolies, Mafia-brand organisations, illicit arms and drug traders, money launderers, pornography merchants, artefact looters and animal thieves—all backed from time to time because they are profitable for someone powerful. No wonder extreme religious regimes make headway. They can claim to be the only ones opposing some of these evils in the name of morality, unfortunately all too often only by imposing illiberal and brutal prescriptions of their own.

At the very least education should be an activity that exists to question the world economic system we have so uncritically accepted as inevitable, in contrast to several other eras in our history, when it has been easier to question, and where major political parties were prepared to differ much more fundamentally.

Thought can change the human condition

First we have to relearn the truth that nothing whatsoever is inevitable. Two centuries ago Tom Paine said that 'We have it in our power to begin the world all over again.' (*Common Sense*, 1776). This has also been one of the major contributions of socialist thinking: to make it clear that our socio-economic system was created by human beings and can be modified by human beings. But this can only happen if people are actively thinking, working, and acting by themselves—not waiting for someone else to act or think for them.

That is why the second key to an alternative policy in education is to encourage the spirit and practice of genuine critical enquiry. Questioning of received wisdom has always been at the heart of a healthy education system, and of a healthy culture and society. It should be reinstated in Britain from the earliest years of a child's education to last through to the last adult stage, and applied to every aspect and level of learning.

Things have gone so far in permitting only 'official' thinking on 'official' subjects from 'official' committees to be learned by teachers who have been 'officially' vetted in every aspect of their work, now extending to colleges and universities, that pressing for relief from the arid formulas pervading education at so many levels in the UK could be much easier than we think—especially with a new government and a new lease of democratic life.

To have increasing input to learning not just from top-level think-tanks, quangos and government committees but equally from the millions who teach and learn, and their communities, will be a welcome first step. But the real advance will come when every learner learns to examine what he or she is taught, and learns how to assess its value for themselves as a matter of course.

Reform of work: Another key

Allied to promoting democratic structures and encouraging critical enquiry in teaching and learning, is the development of a new collective intelligence that fosters and rewards collaborative and co-operative effort as well as individual work. This means an assault on an education system narrowly oriented to competition based on rivalry between individuals and individual institutions, and an end to the domination of education as a processing of people from infancy onwards to serve the needs of a hierarchical labour market. For it has always been the division of work outside that has required the superstructure of academic hurdles inside the education system.

Now that work is changing, we can take advantage of the situation to change the way work relates to education and the way education operates. We can start working to end the 'reproductive' nature of education, a system that prepares us for allotted spots in a divided society.

The 20th century has made some strides already in this respect, for there is more leeway than a century ago for theoretical understanding, where everyone can participate in learning, not just scholars or academics. Education for its own sake, as part of the development of the human spirit, has become far more possible for everyone to pursue alongside their daily tasks, no longer just for those at the top with excessive leisure. There is more activity looking for connections between the various fields of knowledge. New information technology facilitates these developments.

Earlier advances are being rolled back, however, as more and more students face narrower and narrower courses, deliberately limiting the scope for theoretical understanding, particularly of the interrelatedness of knowledge. Indeed, the possibility of this essential wholeness is denied by the new ideology of 'post-modernism' that seems to become the orthodoxy in so much higher education.[10]

The latest to lose out are those training to be teachers, where government is attempting to extend 'hands on' experience to the point where critical and theoretical study all but disappear and there is little attempt to seek a larger understanding of the learning process, let alone knowledge of different ways of working. The irony of introducing such an approach for teachers while trying to cast it aside for those involved in production for capitalism's needs, is another example of the latent contradictions inherent in conservatism.

Equally contradictory is conservatism's denigration of a command economy as practised under old communism, where all economic decisions are made at the centre, with the introduction in education of the 'command classroom', where practically nothing is left to the learners and teachers to decide, and 'excellence' is restricted to whatever comes from teaching to the prescriptions devised at the centre.

Reforming work is a social task

Education is a social process as much as an intellectual one; it is about promoting individual and community development. Our needs are wider than our jobs; society's needs are wider than those of the market. The market is a mechanism which has its uses in organising some aspects of supply and demand but it cannot be left as the sole arbiter of the way resources and life's chances are distributed throughout our society. This is particularly so in the field of work which can no longer be seen as the exclusive provenance of employers, where we thank them for 'largesse' in giving us jobs, when their view of what they are doing is employing us to make a profit for their shareholders or themselves.

Jobs can also be looked at as what we provide for ourselves collectively in a society that we govern for ourselves. In some contexts an eye on what is profitable serves a good purpose, but enterprise should also be judged by whether our economic regime produces the services or goods, and undertakes the tasks, that all would acknowledge are needed in a minimally civilised society. It is the role of education and training that equips people to undertake these tasks, along with a community commitment to fund them, using industry and commerce as required.

Society at large must be involved in determining the way work is created, distributed and shared. This means starting with full (but not necessary full-time) employment for everyone. If people have more time from the sharing out of work, provided their pay maintains them at a decent level, they also have more real choice about their own lives and their social, recreational, cultural and educational pursuits. Work itself has to be reformed to give everyone the right to participate in society by contributing to it through work.

Work is thus a social issue. It has to be seen as much more than commitment to individual companies and enterprises judged solely on their profit for owners and shareholders. It has to be judged as well on its worth to society. Some things are more valuable than others and societies should discuss this issue. In some cases the relative value of many commodities can be decided democratically, not left to the manipulation of the market, as, for example, life-saving medicines (which cost pennies to produce but sell for hundreds of times over this price because 'the market' allows it). Capitalism is blind to such considerations and we know its logic is a barrier in the way of dealing with many health and welfare problems. Even its natural supporters will be ready to call a halt in time, if only because large-scale uprising of populations will be demanding so many modifications.

We already know why it makes sense to have a more equitable system, when looking at several studies which show (both within and between nations) that those communities which have managed to narrow the gap between the top and the bottom in terms of living standards and earnings, are not only economically more successful overall but also healthier and better educated than those which continue to tolerate large gaps getting larger.[11] To change means permitting other values and criteria for judging our 'economies' and 'societies' to have far greater weight. Education should be redirected to include this remit as well as to equip people to further their own goals in leisure, recreational and cultural activity.

Education is a part of life, not just 'preparation' for it

Twenty-first century Britain will live through continuing de-industrialisation while the industrialisation of the poorer areas of the world will grow, passing through the phases we will recognise as having gone through ourselves in the last 150 years. The disjunction between the two will be the focus of much of 21st century world politics. It provides an arena that has potential for great conflict, but also for great gains in co-operative activity and mutual support. For example, it gives us an opportunity to exchange knowledge about clean technologies with poorer areas of the world with a rich biodiversity often threatened by inappropriate development. Education not only should provide us with the means to encourage the co-operative activity and reduce the prospect of conflict; these should be among the prime aims of education.

Education is there to meet the needs of individuals, communities and society as a whole. This is not the same as preparing people for life, educating for the labour market or ensuring ideological quiescence. In these respects we must also reject the idea of education being confined to 'early life preparation'. The 21st century will require education that can operate as a continuously available facility for us to use, when we need it individually, and when society needs it collectively, regardless of a community's status, or anyone's previous qualifications or age.

Thus the majority of education after 18 in the future will inevitably be part-time, enabling people to fit it into their lives naturally, as they develop their interests or talents; or to learn while they work, or bring up their families, interspersed with weeks or terms of continuous intensive study, but without this necessarily being the norm. In particular, the idea that post-18 education to first degree level must any more conform to the pattern of an extension of 'boarding' education for traditional middle class youth sent away from home, is already being challenged, since almost half of those entering much of higher education now are mature students with experience of jobs or families and living at home. Although for everyone in education a period away, in this country or abroad, should be a right anyone can claim at some stage in their educational life, to give them valuable new perspectives, for most people most of the time education will be locally based and part-time.

Extending participation

Genuine life-long education in a redesigned system is what will come to be demanded. This will mean a public service that allows learners to direct themselves, and act on their own initiatives, to organise their own learning much more easily than is now possible, where first you must 'apply' to an institution or a course and then 'get accepted'. People should be encouraged to organise their own teaching, take their own qualifications and go on courses when they deem themselves ready— without getting 'permission' from professional patrons. Teachers have to get ready to add a new role, that of acting as available facilitators, advocators, and providers of learning materials, not just class and lecture hall based instructors hired to teach set courses.

In the 20th century we have often equated 'education' with 'schooling' and with preparing our children for life. In the 21st century we will have to get used to the idea that the education of adults is a major, not a minor, part of education; and to the idea that schooling is only a part of the education of children. More and more parents and grandparents will be actively engaged in education and through this will actively participate in the education of their children. In consequence the role of the family in the education process will evolve and the home-school relationship will take new forms.

At the other end of life the next century will not only see adults engaging *en masse* in learning but also many who are elderly. Hitherto education for the elderly has been relegated to recreational status because life after retirement was thought of as a period of full-time holiday and 'well-earned' rest. But now that many such lives will last for thirty years, there has to be substantial support for a wide variety of educational activity, including assistance in adapting declining skills. Too many older people seem to die of loneliness and boredom and present a major social challenge that education should take its part in meeting.

60009

New goals of social justice and planetary survival

If education is properly ordered and life-long, our obsession with controlling the years of compulsory education, which has dominated education politically for much of this century, will become much less urgent. But if we are to move on from the conservative commitment to economic and ideological reproduction of capital, progressive forces also need to move on from some of their own old Utopian objectives. There is no perfect state or education system, and trying to devise either gets in the way of serving the common good through 'common sense'. As the 21st century continues, social justice and human survival have to be our goals. From primary class through post-degree level work, they are appropriate new concerns for education that could revolutionise the way we teach and learn as well as condition what we learn (not to mention how we organise our society).

Compulsory education was the product of an early capitalist industrialisation that required the mass of people to be a little bit better educated—not fully educated, by any means, just able to undertake the more complex tasks industry required. The same mentality prevails today in exhortations to improve the mass level of technological skill and qualifications and so render advanced capitalist societies 'successful' in the same way. This is what cries to make Britain 'competitive' are all about.

But for what? For the ever escalating polarisation of society that we are seeing in our 'advanced' countries (as well as in those emerging from rural economies)? That is the outcome of unrestrained competition, as we can deduce already. We can see how it leads to more conflict, not less; we can see how it endangers the planet and our survival more each year, rather than protecting either. Just as we have always seen the way it renders large numbers helpless to help themselves, while others prosper.

We have to go beyond goals of increased funding and equality in the existing system, beyond better salaries or defending comprehensive education. Our prescription for the future is to tackle economic inequalities as part of our protection of the planet and its populations—not just the former, as so many 'liberal' or 'conservative' environmentalists propose.

For without social justice, striving for a 'saved' planet will have little meaning when it has been saved.

Taking responsibility for developing ourselves

Education is about the purposes and concerns of the society in all the fields where people are active—culturally, productively, scientifically, and socially. Once we have acquired the basics, education should be about what we collectively and individually decide to learn for ourselves. It will always involve dialogue. Society's job is not to prescribe our thinking and discipline us for roles in one kind of system, but to make it possible for us to carry out the task of developing ourselves, our families and our communities according to criteria which we ourselves have a hand in developing, and within a social context which we have been able to influence through the democratic process.

For example, within a national health service we have to make it possible for people to take a greater hand in the management of their own health and general welfare rather than rely exclusively on authority to prescribe as well as provide. We all must take much more responsibility for our own individual wellbeing. If we are allowed the means to take care of ourselves most people will learn to do so. If we wish to kick the so-called dependency culture, it cannot be done by depriving the deprived even more. It will come only by giving people much more scope to meet their own needs for themselves.

If we are to end education as a mechanism whose main objective is to produce labour hierarchies for a market economy, and make it a real entitlement that puts the social purposes of society as a determining factor, we must break the tie to a culture that expects those considered our 'betters and wisers' to take the major responsibility for our learning, leaving us with no option but fitting into the culture of provision of services and goods that others desire to 'sell' us—both from the public provision as well as within the commercial world. To make a start requires that in education, as indeed, in health, housing, transport, culture and social welfare, we should rethink the whole basis of our social entitlements and the way they are organised, administered and funded.

Education in the 21st century will be about change and planning for it, including planning for life where most people's work will alter many times over, and may rarely be full time. Whether this is good or bad depends upon whether the work is fulfilling and whether there is enough for everyone to be able to sustain themselves. If there is enough, millions of human lives will be open to far fuller development with less work to do. It is the social and economic context in which we experience change that will condition the success or failure of adjusting to the future.

This is why we have to reject the destructively competitive ways of working in a system that will always seek to harness change, and people's flexibility, to blind profit and which relies for success on disciplining the world into winners and losers, those with a lot and those with little, those with sustainable lives and those struggling to eat, instead of devising a system that enables what there is to be shared in some more equitable way.

We have to reject its counterpart within the education system, for any system that requires so large a number of failures, so many who are bored or disruptive, is flawed and wasteful and we know it—just as we know it is deep within the human condition to wish to learn, create and discover and to want to improve our lot in life.

Systems operating on the basis that all can enjoy their basic human rights to succeed in learning are the only ones to postulate as a future for human beings. Any future based on winners and losers or any education system based on a league table mentality, either globally or in our own neighbourhoods, is unsustainable, no matter how high the level of expenditure, how modern the technology or how effective the management.

Towards a society of social entitlement

We still talk of the UK education system as if it existed alone, or occasionally, as part of Europe. But in the 21st century debates and choices will increasingly involve the interaction of each region or nation with many others. The capacity to recognise this interdependence and to plan within a world where the same criteria will one day have to apply to everyone's basic needs and entitlements, regardless of their culture or state of development, will require a flexibility, open-mindedness and problem-solving capacity from education that is far greater than any system currently produces in any culture. There is no reason, however, why Britain could not take a lead in this.

Problem-solving and flexibility are essential for the development of a social entitlement, just as they are essential for those who wish to exploit society for profit, or retain a privileged position, or commandeer a disproportionate share of wealth or power. Every business guru tells us so. Thus the struggle will be between a system where working people (including the self-employed and the small entrepreneur) are using such skills for themselves, as earners, against a system that benefits mainly owners, whether they work or not, including the non-elected corporate employers or the large passive and socially-unconcerned shareholders. Just as wealth does not actually 'trickle down', neither does responsibility for equitable development.

Yet the will to creativity and productivity, to benefit others as well as ourselves, lives in most human beings, and our education alternative would cultivate these fully. That is why we require a policy for rewarding enterprise and learning that fosters understanding and enhances the creative and scientific advances that human beings are capable of making. The present sociopolitical system encourages competitive greed—which is not the same; it also encourages indifference to many forms of oppression and illegality where these conflict with profit-making. Such a system cannot be the only one we allow to undertake the social and democratic and planetary tasks of the future.

That is why a new set of values and a new political imperative are required, a view socialists have always taken, and a view which we believe is now coming to be realised independently by many others, disturbed by growing inequalities and the lack of choice of alternatives for future economic and social development.

Encouraging the growth of new values in society—a new culture of learning for new ends—would not be easy. Resistance will be constant from those with power and empires to lose. But not all of them will be wholly indifferent to the need for some fundamental change in the way society operates. Education is where we start by making it natural to think about the ways in which society can be fundamentally changed rather than just 'managed' better.

Debating a variety of alternative world systems should become a natural part of education. The education system in the UK has come of age and is well able to undertake the task of reshaping itself in the interests of an equitable and democratic society that will play its part in ensuring the survival of both humanity and the natural world in all their diversity. Even if unlikely to be achieved without great struggle, all are worthy goals for the 21st century.

Section III
A NEW CULTURE OF SOCIAL ENTITLEMENT

New educational rights for a new age.

We argue in this book for a new set of rights in education, to be part of a new culture of social entitlement. This culture is being built, not only in education but in fields like health care, social support, housing, environmental protection, transport and the world of useful work. We should continue to discuss the new culture and win support for it by distinguishing it from the old. For example, full employment as defined for forty years after 1945 as every adult male working 40 plus hours a week at a job that remained the same from 16 to 65, is no longer an option. But work for everyone is entirely possible. Indeed, any society that merits the name 'civilised' will make it possible for everyone to contribute to society through work, which brings them enough to live on and support dependants. Society should also make it possible for work to be personally satisfying and for any community's basic needs and services to be met.

But first we have to generate discussion which exposes assumptions and examines practices that have not been examined for decades. We have to try to generate new thinking about education amongst our political leaders and colleagues, amongst our adult population and amongst students and the parents whose children attend our schools. The main objective would be to change the climate of thinking about education which will raise people's own educational sights for themselves, their children and their communities.

Dealing with inequality

Several major changes need to precede new future development. The first is getting to grips with inequality in the present education system.

In recent years the sharp increase in economic, social and political inequality in society at large has been accompanied by an increasing emphasis on economic considerations in education—on 'value for money', ostensibly measured in financial terms. The growing polarisation within the education system mirrors and reinforces the polarisation in society itself. Education thus continues to be not only one of the major results of economic inequality but—because of its growing importance, one of the main causes as well.

Yet issues of equality have virtually disappeared from official education agendas at both local and national level.

The new culture must insist on the principle of equal rights to education, as we insist on equal rights to health care and security. This is one of the foundation stones of our programme for the future. Its significance is that, whilst acknowledging that social and economic considerations will come into play, these must not be allowed to override fundamental concerns with the individual or with society as a whole.

The human need for education is universal and continuing: there is no category of people who have 'no need' of education, nor is there an age when this need ends. No-one can be written off as ineducable. Yet our system as run at present silently accepts such assumptions.

Changing the culture means encouraging everyone to regard education as having an important part to play in every life: Not, however, as in the past, more important for the young or for those who are sure-fire educational 'successes', but in future equally so for society's failures and education's dropouts or for the re-employment prospects of many who have become redundant in consequence of economic change that is no fault of their own. Education is needed to help the elderly to adapt and retain the skills which education offered in their youth, and it is needed by parents to bring up their children.

Beyond compulsory education

Our belief in comprehensive education is not based on the principle that everyone should be the same or that we should try by education to make people alike but from our fundamental concern that no accidents of birth or environment and no personal characteristics should be permitted, as they are now, to ensure privileged access to the education from which all individuals could and should benefit.

At first sight this may seem like the reassertion of a well-established principle but it is not one that has hitherto formed the basis of our educational system. We have many pious statements about not discriminating on lines of 'race', gender or disability (with rather fewer for class or sexuality) but the principle set out above has not been the basis of policies and reforms introduced by any British government.

There has been some recognition of universal educational needs of people between the ages of five and sixteen (along with per capita funding of school education, at least in theory). But in the provision for the other age groups, including pre-school and post-school students, there has not even been lip service paid to equality; and in practice there are huge variations which no-one has ever attempted to justify or even rationalise. Thus for many young children and adults there is no educational provision whatsoever.

Most current discussion centres on the compulsory years of education when everyone is supposedly within the system. The new culture of education has to move from fixation on compulsory learning by giving equal attention to education where participation is voluntary—where people can seek education because they want it or need it for their lives or the life of their community.

Employing everyone as the basis for social justice

In Britain we cling to outdated thinking about the economic needs of education. One of its components is the 'quick fix' which governments have eagerly pursued in one 'new deal' after another, for example, to provide training in useful skills for the under-educated and unemployed. As nearly 30 trials have shown, this model does not work for the majority involved for two reasons: it does not meet society's economic need and it does not meet the needs of the people concerned. Even President Clinton and his conservative advisors have accepted that a compliant unskilled workforce led by a highly educated body of technocrats is an idea of the past. For a modern advanced economy (regardless of its political direction) having a large sector of the workforce that is uneducated practically ensures unemployment for increasing numbers.

The 'quick fix' may have some short-term benefit in terms of creating a few training places or work placements (often displacing employed workers to create them) but it has notably failed to improve the quality of the jobs or the general level of skill in the workforce. If it is enforced (e.g. through benefit withdrawal) it damages future work relations and commitment to the community for significant sectors of the population. This is one example of the way in which short-term thinking is holding back Britain's economic development relative to that of other countries with a more education-based approach.

No minor reform will correct this. Running throughout the British education system is the idea of selection and segregation of those, always a minority, deemed worthy of substantial education and career support (often for careers that can be guaranteed). They are segregated (often literally) from a majority deemed worthy of basic education and training only. A good proportion (but not all) of the majority gets some form of job, but no more and certainly not a secure career, the goal towards which so many in previous generations were willing to work. Others in this second group get nothing at all.

A measure of the prevailing inequality which we have identified is the extent to which it is assumed by the traditional middle classes and those who have obtained their education, that their children will be in the first of these two groups and that the public system of education, with possibly some contribution from the private sector, will facilitate this. In sharp contrast with the assumption that most boys and girls from the council housing estates, depressed areas and inner cities will leave school at 16 and look for a lower level job. Despite lip service to the contrary, society accepts their perception that universities and colleges have little to do with them.

All the way through—in selection, admissions legislation, pupil grouping, examinations, course construction, and funding—the mechanisms of education are set up to ensure that more gets given to those who already have great advantages, whether institutions or individuals. There is an almost unchallenged assumption that only some people need education beyond eighteen and that priority must be given to the 'most able' minority, who in practice turn out to include most of the offspring of the prosperous. These unchallenged assumptions, which lie at the heart of the two nations, colour and determine the whole education system.

Equality of opportunity has not worked, despite the fact that it remains an ever popular theme. It is true that an exceptional child from the poorest home may do well at school and proceed to a university and a successful career. But it is also true that the cards are as heavily stacked as ever against young people from the 'bottom 50 per cent' of society.

Redistributing resources and opportunities through the extension of the comprehensive principle

Our problem is not solved merely by providing the opportunity. Opportunity must be provided in such a form and in such a context and climate that all are able to make full use of it.

In the health field, for example, we are not satisfied that the opportunity exists for vaccination or cancer screening. A socially effective policy organises to make sure that everyone at risk takes advantage of what is available. Education policy must also ensure that everyone takes advantage of the educational opportunities available by organising to ensure that this happens. Ignorance and incompetence are as avoidable as diseases.

The 19th century saw a long drawn-out struggle for the comprehensive principle in respect of elementary education for everyone. In the 20th century the main struggle has been for comprehensive education at the secondary stage. The 21st century will see that struggle extend beyond the age of 16/18 right to the end of life.

In the course of these two historic struggles over 200 years, we have learned that true equality has to be inclusive and dynamic, and encompass the whole process of challenging inequality that arises through 'race', gender, class, sexuality, disability and age.[12] It is important to recognise that in practice any oppression that manifests itself as a single factor, will, on closer examination, be seen as multidimensional. The effects of each impact upon all of the others. We must avoid examining each kind of oppression in isolation for that leads only to a hierarchy of oppressions marginalising other.

But there are further inequalities which have not been tackled in the same way, that is in terms of organising resistance to them. Public expenditure on education cannot be unlimited and any case for increasing it will require justification against competing claims from housing or health or transport. In a context in which emphasis is placed on using public expenditure to redress social inequality, the claim of education will be unconvincing so long as the effect of education is towards increasing social inequality.

Redistribute expenditure

There is therefore an urgent need to review the pattern of educational expenditure, not just to ensure efficiency and effectiveness, but also to review priorities. As well as pressing for more funding overall, we have to re-examine the way resources are distributed and seek to redistribute them on a new and more socially just basis.

In recent years some efforts have been made to do this but they have generally failed as a consequence of reluctance to challenge many traditional practices and assumptions, including widespread and hidden institutional selection. Notable too is the blanket assumption that the older the student and the more advanced the study the more expensive it should be, that in the education system there is an inevitable hierarchy of institutions and teachers starting with universities at the top and nurseries at the bottom. While there is undoubtedly some basis for some aspects of this assumption, in that higher education sometimes requires expensive equipment or teaching with specialist expertise, this is not the whole story by any means.

There is, for example, widespread acceptance that teaching at secondary level demands significantly higher level of resources than at primary level, in either materials or staffing. This assumption is derived from historical antecedents of the primary schools as part of the 'elementary' system for the poor and the secondary schools as a system for the more well-to-do. It needs to be challenged.

The inequalities of provision are even more extreme in the post-school sector. For many after 18 there is no provision whatsoever and for others the provision is lavish. The lion's share of this goes on the education of the 'academically successful' minority who proceed to higher education. The justification for restricting education in this way is far from clear—other than that it has always been done and is practised elsewhere in the world. But it is precisely in those economically advanced countries like Britain that this assumption must now come into question, not just in the name of equality but in the name of raising those all-round standards in society that apply to everyone at every stage in life.

End 18-plus selection

The Further Education Funding Council's (FEFC) Report on widening participation, *Learning Works*, (1997), marked a turn of the tide by pointing out the inequitable funding of post-16 education and recommending a better balanced spending division between the 'privileged' sixth forms and universities, on the one hand, and the further education colleges on the other. Earlier, it was the Labour Party's Borrie Commission which recognised the same problem when it stated that 'Funding adult learning on an equitable basis, with no discrimination between different types of learning' had to be considered (*Commission for Social Justice*, p. 141). This same Commission also offered the figure that student grants for students living away from home are worth ten times as much to the richest 20 per cent of families as they are to the poorest 20 per cent (ibid. pp. 137/8).

But the problem is not merely spending three times as much on the higher education student as on a student in further education or requiring the latter (generally less well-off) to pay fees while for decades higher education students had 'free' education through state grants

For our argument, it is not even a question of whether the proportion of people who are 'suitable' for higher education should be raised from

30 per cent to 50 per cent or why teaching in further and adult education is considered a job whereas teaching in more than one centre of higher education is considered as incidental employment for those who regard themselves as primarily interested in research; or why academic freedom is considered essential in higher education but not necessarily elsewhere.

The essential question is whether there is any justification for continuing to regard higher education as a distinct sector of education and why it should not be incorporated with further and adult education into a comprehensive system of provision for all adults after 18 where the enormous diversity of needs and paths can be managed equitably? The greater pressure which society needs to bring to bear to increase the funding coming to public education throughout the system, will be compromised while such an inequitable system remains unquestioned.

The existing system ensures massive socially regressive expenditure on post-school education, spending vast sums of public money on strengthening the social and economic advantages of those who are already advantaged by birth, home and schooling. With, by comparison, pittance expenditure for the rest of the registered students after 18 in Britain, who are not in the universities, let alone the ancient ones, but in the colleges of further and adult education.

The inequalities are gross and the remedies are simple in principle but remarkably difficult in practice because power in this and other 'advanced' countries is held largely by those who, along with their children, are the beneficiaries of the present inequitable system. Getting more money overall into education, essential as this is, cannot remain the solitary goal; it has to go hand in hand with more equitable distribution.

Deal with needs-blind funding

Conservative governments did us a service by highlighting the significance of private contributions to the education of children while arriving at the wrong conclusions. Schooling is only a part of a child's education and cannot be considered in isolation from the education obtained outside school—in the home and amongst playmates.

The conservative response to this is to see allocation of children to schooling that is in the style of the home, basic for the poor but with better basics–plus extras, for the more prosperous. Our response is that equity demands compensation in school for educational deficiency at home. To put it bluntly, we require more generous financial provision, of both revenue and capital, for the schooling of the poor than for that of the rich. A conservative policy has been used relentlessly to engineer the opposite.

Conservative ideas of equity also involve a policy of 'needs–blind' funding, a mechanism clearly intended to ignore the claims of democracy as well as to fuel continued polarisation of the system. For under legislation since 1979 (returning selection, open enrolment, 'specialisation' and engineered 'choice'), a minority of institutions are rewarded and encouraged to flourish, while at the other end a minority are set up to die by league-table attrition. Acting tough with a few of these does little for the condition of many in between, which merely exist close to the edge.

Social factors that affect performance may multiply (like high turnover and large percentages taking free meals) but the funding mechanism is not designed to cope. And now the same principle is being spread to colleges and universities. A new superstructure of privilege is being built, with public funding, as the semi–privatisation of the state sector complements (and protects) the state subsidisation of the private sector.

To prevent democratic redress by local people the law has allowed schools to opt out of local democratic structures and it has allowed all further education colleges and higher education institutions to be 'independent' of their communities as well, with ever more encouragement to disengage themselves from democratic accountability to a locally elected community or regional authority. This too is justified by pseudo–egalitarian needs–blind funding—e.g., 'a common funding formula will ... insulate (GM) schools from the decision of an (elected) authority'.[13] How isolation from the democratic process for some but not for others, assists education to serve all citizens equally, has yet to be explained.

Deal with inequality of choice

It is essential in a free society that people can make choices, in education as elsewhere. But the current practice of 'choice' is a travesty of this principle, being narrowly confined to secondary education as well as disproportionately to parents with private means or to the educationally advantaged whose children get 'chosen' for selective education or the better funded school.

Choice is an issue much wider than institutional preference at the secondary stage. It is also a major issue for all adults after 18. It is an issue for children as well. For example, in the mandatory school curriculum, could more curriculum choice be accorded to children as well as parents, thus embodying one of the most difficult problems that confronts us in schooling. How much learning is to be required in the school curriculum for the good of society as a whole and how much is to be left free to individual choice?

These are democratic decisions that apply at every stage of education, that communities should be involved in making sure are fair, open and honest—which is far from the case at present. In addition, there are a host of areas in education, relating to gender, 'race', religion, class, sexuality, disability and locality, where issues of choice should be negotiated in every community on a continuing basis. But how often is this the case?

Our greatest concern should be with forms of choice presented dishonestly in that there is disregard of the disadvantage for some that inevitably flows from the privilege granted to others. To take but one example, to continue to argue the rights for parents to 'choose' grammar schools assumes that most parents prefer secondary modern schools, when, clearly, there is no evidence for this. Governments' protection of grammar 'choice' has been a protection for a minority of parents to choose mainly white traditionally middle-class schools. This has now extended to the freedom of some schools (but not the majority) to 'choose' their pupils under open enrolment—which inevitably turn out to be weighted with children from 'good' homes. If those chosen are Asian, black or from other minority ethnic communities, they are likely to be stable and aspiring—not newly arrived refugees whose command of English is as yet imperfect (Benn and Chitty, 1996, Chapters 3 and 4).

Class snobbery and self interest cannot be eliminated in society but communities should ensure that neither is given legitimacy in shaping the system by insuring fairness in the admissions process and the provision of facilities, as well as in the extra provision of resources where needs are greatest. In the immediate future admissions to secondary schools, for example, are in such a state of chaos and opacity that some reform is inevitable. (In the longer term the siting and sizes of schools and colleges and the policy for housing and the way it is distributed, are matters with which society must concern itself through the democratic process. At present this type of 'planning' barely exists or where it does, defers to commercial developers' interests.)

Rights to access and provision

Hitherto people in Britain have had few established rights in education. Normal expectations have grown but many of these, such as the existence of a reasonably accessible school or public library, have been so eroded in recent years that they should now be formally established and expanded in recognition of modern needs and expectations.

Certain provision and certain access should be guaranteed by law and should be untainted by unfair discrimination. The United Kingdom has legislation outlawing discrimination on grounds of sex, disability and 'race' (except in Northern Ireland) and religion (only in Northern Ireland). Some of this applies to access to places and opportunities in education. Fairness of educational choice should be promoted by substantially strengthening equal opportunities legislation, both generally and in relation to education.

'Race' and sex and disability discrimination in the allocation of educational places and opportunities are already outlawed. This legislation should be extended to discrimination on social, religious and sexuality grounds and should include indirect as well as direct discrimination. This should also include ending selection for education on grounds of prior academic attainments, and this should be made explicit. It would not guarantee completely open access to educational places (just as employment law does not guarantee open access to jobs) but it would severely constrain the grounds on which access could be refused and selection justified.

In respect of post-school education the principles of open access to facilities and fairness in access to other services and further rights in the neighbourhood college and university, should be guaranteed by legislation. This would include rights of access of adults to many local educational premises like colleges and universities during hours and times that do not interfere with the work already taking place there.

More difficult to overcome than individual discrimination is the problem of structural discrimination. Rights of access to facilities and services and courses are of little use if these are not effectively available. There must be new consideration and legislation about the statutory provision to be made in respect of responsible bodies of national, regional and local government to ensure educational opportunities are effectively available to all. This must include accessible nursery care and education for all; updated standards of provision for both children and adults with special needs; new and more liberal standards about reasonable travelling distance for infants, children and adults and a re-examination of statutory provision of transport for those in need; and, for the first time, some guarantee of educational provision for adults.

Right to a named local school

One right is urgent and that is the right to attend a named local school at all stages of education from nursery onwards (and in time a named local further education college or the satellite classes of local universities). This is a right many countries already ensure, based on the widespread knowledge that local people are better able to support local institutions and that support from their communities is essential for local institutions. In the UK a parent has no rights to enter a school even if the family lives next door. Recent legal changes have seen local people displaced by those coming in from outside who have exercised 'choice', with those displaced sent to schools they did not choose in communities where they do not live.

In Bromley, for example, where selection has spread to almost every school, hundreds of pupils in any one year will have been unable to find a place in schools in their own area. This is an extreme case, of course, a new situation where a 'grammar' authority (into which the more affluent bus their children) is surrounded by several 'secondary modern' authorities. But dozens of areas share the same difficulty in a national admissions system which many researchers, including the Audit Commission, has found gravely defective.[14]

Giving every child a school of right does not mean the parent must accept it. The same rules which apply to expressing a preference could still apply, with schools required to honour it where they have room (provided no child whose school of right it is, gets displaced). Such legislation would not only strengthen the local bond to schools in communities, especially as it is now obvious that the 'neighbourhood' school or college is a popular concept. It would also reduce the need for such a vast and costly oversupply of school places. As parents have come to realise that 'parental choice' is really 'selective schools' choice', groups throughout the country are organising to support alternative admissions systems, including rights to use their local school.

End 'market' competition to extend choice

At the same time choice in other aspects of education, currently denied to many students because competition has been enforced, can be ensured. This applies particularly to 15 and 16 year olds choosing their courses for the year in any area. At present many, if not most, institutions proceed by jealously guarding their students, often keeping them from knowledge about courses in other local institutions. Far from competition guaranteeing choice, it seems clear that competition has become the enemy of choice.

Until the sum total of courses in any one area is available for choice to all who live in the area (and students' choice is not restricted by the schools and colleges where they happen to be enrolled nor schools penalised when an enrolled students take some of their study elsewhere) the system will continue to deny choice to large numbers. A few local areas (like Oxford) have already pioneered a pooled system between schools' sixth forms, sixth form colleges and further education (with funding fairly apportioned between all institutions). Institutions in a few large cities are soon to co-operate at this stage. Yet no one has studied 'good practice' in this vital area and made it available, much less given such ventures the legislative and government support they require.

There should be statutory guarantees of a minimum available curriculum at every stage, and of materials and facilities. In addition to a basic curriculum for those of school and nursery age (which would be common within any institution), there must be guarantees of educational and careers advice for people of all ages; training and assistance towards employment and re-employment; restart basic education for adults; educational training assistance for groups like carers and former carers seeking re-entry to the labour market; and educational and training support for the elderly.

But 16-19 is a priority. There should be specific statutory provision, including subsistence support if necessary, for the education and training of everyone between the ages of 16 and 18. This should be reinforced by a statutory limitation of the weekly working hours to not more than 20 and backed up by a school or college of right within the local or regional authority. The local authority should have a specific responsibility for overseeing the education and training of every young person in this age group who wants to stay in state-funded training or education, full or part-time. At present it is only those who are full-time in schools who get this attention.

Rights to work towards a qualification

The most important changes in the long run, however, will be those freeing up the system so that people can use it more easily. For most people an important benefit of education is the achievement of a qualification by passing an examination or completing a course. Rights of access to models of assessment are therefore important and must not be impeded by imposing elaborate preconditions such as attendance at classes, membership of institutions or passing of previous examinations.

In time it might even be unlawful to prevent any individual, on any grounds whatsoever, from taking any examination. That includes all institutions and professional bodies. All forms of examinations and tests should be fair and seen to be fair and all examiners and examining bodies made publicly accountable for their competence and submit themselves to annual independent audit of examining and certification.

Rights like those listed, however, require a change of climate in education, moving away from the idea that someone else educates you if you are lucky enough to enter the right door, to one where people understand that they have to take a much larger part in educating themselves and their children, and actively engage in making use of the public education system and its resources to do so, rather than waiting for someone else to give them their education.

We must move away from the idea of being consumers of education to being 'producers of knowledge'.

Rights to funding for groups and individuals: Basic social income

Rights to funding in order to study is another essential commitment. Indeed, the key to rights lies in funding, for without a drastic reordering of the economic foundation of learning, universal rights will not be realisable. Nor will it be possible to establish education as a true public service that will be available to everyone at every age.

To undertake the change required involves abandoning the idea that education is mainly about children to realise that it is about people of every age. We have not begun to take the implications of this coming sea-change on board. The mass education of adults requires all the other changes we are suggesting, including taking more responsibility for our own learning, and of learning in new contexts and by new means.

But it also requires a new and far simpler social security system, where basic support is available throughout life for those in society for whom nothing else is available. It would include those in this position who are studying after 16 and up to the end of life.

Hillcole has already recommended scrapping all grants and loans in education, as part of a new and far simpler social security system overall. This would include a basic social income for everyone in society over the age of 16, available only to those who had no other income or means of support (Hillcole, 1991, Chapter 8). It would thus exclude those who were at work, on a pension, on unemployment benefit, or those from a household with an income from work.

A short compulsory period of 5-16 education would be funded by the community, as would the period up to 18. But thereafter the Education Service would be available to all adults on the same basis. This would have to be an affordable basis. Thus all would pay user-charges based on the progressive principle of a nationally agreed and fixed percentage of their income or the income of their household—with national provision providing safeguards for communities in particular situations, e.g. rural areas or those particularly neglected. Those whose only source of income was the basic social income could not be charged for any education at any stage, including higher degree education.

Those with paying jobs, pensions or the income of parents or partners would contribute according to levels that were genuinely affordable (agreed through the democratic process). It is not user charges that enrage people, who are, after all, used to paying them in further and adult education. It is excessive charges that price the learning out of the range of those on modest incomes; or making the poor pay the same as the rich, or making the poor subsidise the rich through loans and fee-paying. Or even worse, using the principle of charges to undermine a public education service over time by continually raising them in order to privatise education.

To be affordable means educational charges after 18 being affordable to each individual, without causing hardship to them or their families; and without the iniquities and bureaucracy of the old means-testing by making it possible for those in learning to undertake their own assessment of charges due. This would accompany a system that provided a coherent and equitably organised funding of courses—not according to the status of the institution but according to the nature of the course.

With these basics in place, the idea of life-long education — the '*education permanente*' originally envisaged by socialists in France[15] — will start to become a reality. Everyone will be entitled to funding for education for themselves or their children throughout life, to be taken when they chose. Not in lavish style after 18, perhaps, but an improvement on a system that gives substantial support where the majority of individuals or families are reasonably secure or affluent but puts others deep into debt, or turns them away entirely. In this connection it would be necessary to consider transferring some of our heavy military expenditure to support education and training as well as to consider a renewed commitment to progressive taxation as a way of helping ensure essential public services including education.

We make no claim that our approach would be without problems but a start would be made on an adequate financial base and for the first time to ensure that the money available would be distributed equitably. For such a radical policy to succeed, however, requires an equally radical revision and simplification of all public entitlements. In return for the new contribution people would be expected to make towards their own learning would go many more rights in respect of that learning.

Releasing the popular will to learn

The key to the idea of a new National Education Service is that adults should take increasing responsibility for their own learning (and that of their children) with a publicly funded service there to help them do this rather than a system which allocates 'chances' according to socially biased and archaic legal and fiscal formulas. No longer should the general public be treated as childlike recipients of teaching or as citizens unable to appreciate the finer points of curriculum, testing, funding, or research at national level. Their primary need for themselves is access to knowledge and facilities; it is not just to be provided with classrooms and teachers. Their primary need in respect of their children is access to all the facts relating to the education service and assurances that resources and opportunities will be equally available for them.

We do not follow fashion in talking of education as a 'business'. As it has often been used in recent times, the idea is absurdly and dangerously simplistic. Human rights cannot be reduced to a balance sheet covered by a business plan. Good management is essential because the funds are the public's, but profit in education can never be measured in monetary terms. There have to be clear social criteria for education as a human right that cannot be bought and sold.

Fiscal probity and value for money can apply successfully to the public services only when decisions on the distribution of all resources are open to public debate, and expenditure is totally accountable to the democratically elected. Accountability of this kind has been severely eroded in the last two decades and should be reinstated as a matter of urgency.

Rights are not what you are given but what you already have. Education is one of them. A new culture of education must start from this point.

SECTION IV
APPLYING ALTERNATIVE PRINCIPLES TO TODAY'S POLICY

A. Curriculum, assessment, and teaching

So far we have discussed the long-term re-orientation of education required in the context of expected social, economic and technological developments in the 21st century. We turn now to changes required in the more immediate future.

Early years: Education and care combined (not one or the other)

Life-long education is not just about extending learning through adult years. It is also about extending it downwards to the first five years of life.

Not all parents will want their children to be in nursery or pre-school education, but the evidence is that most would welcome this opportunity for at least some time. They would also welcome an experience that combined learning with day care, since it is commonly accepted that the earlier a child is socialised, the better she or he fares later. This is not just academically, but socially as well, as extended research on American Headstart programmes has confirmed. Everyone also knows that many parents, particularly women, want the chance to continue their own working lives while also being parents, and need the support that only early years education and care can give. To this should be added after school and holiday care for older children.

From every point of view, education and childcare going hand in hand, have to be on offer from the very earliest months, as they already are in many other countries. If parents are not working, there is evidence that even young babies benefit from education that alerts parents to the kinds of activities that stimulate their development and stretch their learning. Investment in provision here would undoubtedly bring returns to society greater than in almost any other area of education.

Yet there is no current commitment to undertake a full provision of early years education. The best we have is a plan to extend a nursery place or a pre-school place to those who are aged four, and in time to those aged three. It will no doubt mean a real momentum in improvements for education for these ages, but there are several difficulties. First, there remains the earlier ages, where some parents will continue to want education, support and care for their children. Second, there is a great deal of difference between a full nursery education and a few hours in a pre-school class attached to a local primary school. Just as there is a great deal of difference between a facility that is basically social care and one that is fully educational.

Integration of education and care is the best way to prevent divisions of this nature in future. Many of the *ad hoc* proposals currently on offer do not bring together social care facilities with those of nursery education, providing both for all children. This is a union long overdue, and necessary to end the invidious division of poorer children left in social care (with little education) while better-off parents commit their children to the learning experiences of well-organised (and often costly) nursery schooling.

The nursery voucher experiment proved a disaster—inefficient, costly, inequitable and failing the majority—largely because the scheme had hidden objectives in addition to its ostensible motive to extend education. The first was to subsidise the private sector and the second was to keep spending on public nursery education down. In the event, these cancelled each other out.

Failure also attended voucher systems at secondary level (tried and abandoned in parts of Kent in 1978 where the hidden objective was to make a selective system look equitable but ended when the results showed the cost of subsidising private schooling was exorbitantly expensive for the state). Hardly successful either—in terms of its own goals—have been training schemes based on 'credits', which have involved a wasteful paper chase and no dramatic improvement in the uptake of training.[16]

Pre-5 Education: A chance to involve communities

Reorganising the system to provide for universal availability of nursery schooling for ages 3 and 4, and to ensure it is integrated with day care, is only a start. During the reorganisation, attention needs to be given to the many ways in which the forms of existing care and education are supported and extended, with new forms added. There are many models that can be used and variety in this respect is essential, provided the principles of non-selective access and true affordability for all sections of the community are scrupulously observed.

A drive for education for pre-school children is a change that could benefit the whole community by involving it in the work of developing facilities and activities generally, including educational facilities for adults. The whole process must also be seen as a chance for adults to extend their own education too. Parents or grandparents in areas where needs are greatest can be encouraged to undertake the work of running some of the new provision themselves. Training for them could be provided, along with training in other fields like managing of housing estates or providing greater opportunities for sport, in ways that residents in any area could use to improve the life of their neighbourhood. The same approach could be extended to after school and holiday care for older school children. At present it seems to be the intention to rely too heavily on charities to undertake this work, which means some areas get provision and others do not. That is the great drawback to the 'voluntary' approach to universal rights.

B. Pedagogy: What type of teaching?

The type of teaching given in the early years, including, of course, the primary years is currently under debate. The current vogue is for yet another return to basics, taught formally and strictly, at least in terms of the three Rs. Some in the new government seem as keen on this approach as the old was to rule out 'progressive' teaching styles. But what are these? No-one seems to know for sure.

There is much confusion and uncertainty on the matter because there has been a politically driven debate designed to misrepresent what happens, particularly in primary schools. Research shows that in the vast majority of primary schools, a mixture of methods is used. It is also clear that over many years a considerable body of experience and expertise has been built up which now governs primary school practice using this mixture.

What can be discussed is poor teaching, of course, but this is just as likely to be a feature of traditional methods as it is of progressive ones. The important point here is that low attainment in education is far less often due to poor teaching than it is to the result of some aspect of poverty and all that relates to it. Thus to propose a war between child-centred and formal methods without also addressing the context is to be caught up unnecessarily in a narrow argument driven by ideological prejudice and blind to common problems.

In practice, there is very little conflict between methodologies; there is only a common set of practices which is divers and always developing. Some was initiated once upon a time by Plowden, perhaps, but not restricted by it: witness the gradual abandonment of Piagetian notions of fixed stages of child development. The reality is that pedagogy in primary schools is and will remain, the work of many hands.

There is plenty of research to back this up, and even now new research that gives us information about the long term effects of different teaching styles in early education, with new information appearing every year. For example, one project, taking youngsters from inner-city backgrounds and following them up to adulthood, compared three methods of early life teaching (traditional, exploratory, and a mixture).[17] Results showed that formally-taught children got an early boost in 3 Rs attainment levels but by age 10 the others had caught up. By aged 23, however, those who had had child-centred pre-school education (which encouraged them to seek out learning experiences that had meaning to them and to follow these up under their own steam) had better academic records as well as more stable lives, than those who had been 'formally' instructed in the early years. The latter also had significantly higher numbers without qualifications and were more likely to be in trouble with the law.

It is always a mistake to back 'one right way' and throw everything else to the winds. Learning has to be something people can make 'their own' if it is to have any meaning for them. Teachers must keep an open mind if they are to convey open-mindedness to learners. Learning cannot be that which is imposed against wills. Instead of gunning for successful teachers who use some elements of child-centred learning in their work, we should be concerned to tackle the narrow pronouncements of those who support the politicisation of OFSTED.

Educating those who teach

Teacher educators throughout the country are busily implementing new course programmes of work designed to meet the requirement for a greater role for schools and teachers in Initial Teacher Education (ITE). Indeed, it is even possible for schools wishing to do so to assume total responsibility for the professional preparation of teachers, where intending teachers have no higher education involvement whatsoever.

The 1994 Education Act removed the funding for teacher education institutions from the Higher Education Funding Council for England (HEFCE) and handed it over to a Teacher Training Agency (TTA), yet another new quango with its members appointed directly by the Secretary of State for Education. Bureaucratic oversight spread and the system took another step towards central government control of education and innovation.

The oversight spreads right down to what is learned, for these changes have introduced, in effect, a National Curriculum for ITE which also effectively marginalises the study of social, political and ideological contexts of schooling. It also marginalises those who teach such courses. The new ITE curriculum is now far more 'technicist' and far less 'critical' than teacher education ought to be. These changes not only risk diminishing educational breadth for young people; they also threaten to reduce teachers from professional to operative status.

It will not be long before college and university teaching are similarly controlled, with threats of a genuine loss not just of critical thinking and academic freedom but of innovative democratic practice as well. It is an irony that a conservative impetus originally so committed to 'independence' and 'freedom' should have ended up so dedicated to establishing a culture of state control and dependence on central directives—as if, somehow, critical thinking could not be left to develop freely.

Good teaching needs a wide, rigorous and balanced education

Many professionals and others who care about education are strongly opposed to the view that preparation to be a teacher, at whatever level, is simply a matter of 'on-the-job training'. That is why the movement to make teacher-training wholly school-based must be regarded as a retrograde step. We have already provided details of our own proposals for Teacher Education in a number of Hillcole Group publications[18], all of which argue that parents, teachers and teacher educators must resist narrow, restrictive competency and skills-based teacher training and insist on the development of critical, reflective teachers and pupils. Teachers need more than subject knowledge and classroom skills. They need to reflect on their own and others' attitudes and actions and which should be taken or avoided. They need to be aware of all the arguments concerning pedagogy—as for example, in the curriculum or in pupil grouping.

In order to be free to innovate as well as to develop professional skills to meet the needs of an ever growing culture of education well beyond the 'traditional' routes students previously encountered, we propose a core curriculum for Initial Teacher Education which includes not only classroom skills and competencies, but also a theoretical understanding of children, schooling and society and their interrelationships, describing alternative views and methods of, for example, classroom organisation and topic selection. In time we would propose the same for those who will be teaching adults over 18.[19]

Teacher educators and their institutions constitute a powerful repository of knowledge, experience and skill in preparing our teachers for a professional career. Teacher educators clearly do not have a monopoly on this knowledge, but any move which marginalises and erodes their work may well present very real difficulties in the future. This is why so many argue for broadening classroom work by adding study in higher education: In the words of Professor John Furlong:

> 'School-based courses give students an in-depth training in one or at best two schools [but]... It is access to this broader perspective that helps students develop an understanding of the principles by which they work...[and] a breadth of perspective is a vital complement to the particularity of training that schools provide. Without access to the broader perspective that higher education can provide, we run the risk of producing a profession that is ever more inward-looking' (Furlong, 1993, p. 14).

We also run the risk of perpetuating costly bias, for

> 'research evidence suggests that many teachers continue, consciously or otherwise, to make important decisions about the organisation, orientation and delivery of the formal and informal curricula on grounds which are racist, sexist and discriminatory in a range of significant ways. Should we, therefore, [not]...develop pre-service courses geared towards the development of a teaching force which reflects in a critical manner on taken-for-granted assumptions, which can articulate reasons for contesting some of the conventional wisdom about pupils, their interest and abilities, and which, ultimately might influence future cohorts?' (Troyna and Sikes, 1993, p. 25)

Such a core curriculum for all who teach in any part of the education system would embrace equality and develop equal opportunities so that children or adults do not suffer from labelling, under-expectation, stereotyping or prejudice from their teachers and lecturers—or, indeed, from their peers. It would also enable student teachers to develop as critical, reflective practitioners, able, for example, to decode official distortion, bias and propaganda and understand why certain practices appear to have official endorsement while others are rejected as subversive or unsound. It is an unsound society that regards everything stemming from government as above critical reflection (Blackman, 1996).

Develop the science of teaching

The 21st century will require much from those who teach—not just in primary and secondary classrooms but in post-18 education centres of every kind. Are these retrograde changes a good enough foundation upon which to build in respect of a profession whose work is going to change out of all recognition in the 21st century?

In an important paper, Brian Simon sought to account for the nonexistence of 'pedagogy', in the sense of the 'science of teaching', in educational discussion in this country (Simon, 1981). He argued that our whole approach to educational theory and practice has tended to be both amateurish and highly pragmatic in character: 'the most striking aspect of current thinking and discussion about education is its eclectic character, reflecting deep confusion of thought, and of aims and purposes, relating to learning and teaching—to pedagogy' (Simon, 1981, p.124).

In seeking likely explanations for this peculiarly English phenomenon, we can refer to the amateurish approach of the country's most prestigious educational institutions, the leading 'public' schools and the ancient universities, as playing a leading part. For much of the last hundred years, it has been considered absurd that a professional training should be in any sense relevant to the task of teaching in a public school; and, until recently, neither Oxford nor Cambridge has made any serious contribution to the development of educational theory and practice in this country.

It is also true that in the interwar years, the emphasis on mental measurement, particularly intelligence testing, served to promote the view that education had little or no role to play in the development of abilities. Psychometrists from the 1930s asserted that human intelligence was fixed, innate and unchangeable, a view that set definable limits to achievement and learning. After the war a leading psychometrist put it that 'in an ideal community, our aim should be to discover what ration of intelligence nature has given to each individual child at birth, then to provide him (sic) with an appropriate education, and finally to guide him into the career for which he seems to have been marked out' (Burt, 1950).

It was this pernicious theory which provided convenient justification for the divided secondary system of the postwar years—and still finds a few adherents within 'respectable' academic circles (see Simon, 1996). More worrying, psychometric testing is increasingly used today in youth training and job selection.

Debate the differences that matter

The legacy of all this is profound confusion about the nature of learning and an undue emphasis (in schooling) on the unresolved dichotomies between 'modern' and 'traditional' approaches, between 'child-centred' and 'subject-centred' approaches, or simply between the 'informal' and the 'formal'. Such categorisations are invariably crude and meaningless but continue to muddy the waters and prevent us from seeing where true differences exist, even among groups in close agreement on most other educational matters.

Within progressive teaching, for example, it is fair to point out that there are broadly two approaches to pedagogy, particularly where primary-school teaching is concerned. On the one hand, there are those who espouse 'child-centred' theories of learning and would probably accept the theoretical or pedagogical stance of the 1967 Plowden Report. On the other, there are those who play down the concept of individual differences and would argue for a greater systematisation and structuring of the child's experiences in the process of learning.

The Plowden Report was a particularly influential document with its emphasis on individual children and their learning needs: 'at the heart of the educational process lies the child'. The Report certainly had a liberating influence on vast numbers of primary-school teachers, and received a warm welcome in many sections of the media. There was broad support for both its child-centred approach and its rejection of fatalistic theory about human potential. It seemed to be generally accepted that individualisation of the educational process was the all-important principle according to which all educational strategies and tactics must henceforth be formulated. And since human development was unpredictable, there was clearly no justification for the categorisation or streaming of children according to their supposed ability at a fixed point in time.

How structured should learning be?

It is difficult, even now, to be critical of Plowden for this is to risk identification with the essentially philistine and atheoretical standpoint of the elitist or rigid traditionalist, for the Report was a popular target of contributors to the early Black Papers and to this day remains a target for many conservatives. Yet there are those on the 'progressive' side who also reject Plowden's 'pedagogic romanticism' and argue that it takes the child-centred approach to indefensible limits. Providing a deficit view of working-class children has focused efforts to equalise opportunity on repairing deficiencies in individual children rather than on structures and curriculum (Epstein, 1993, p. 92).

Others have serious misgivings about the individualisation of the learning process and would propose a more active role for the classroom teacher in the deliberate structuring of a child's activities. This is not to say that they believe it is wrong to make use of co-operative group work as well as individualised activities, simply that these must always be designed and structured in relation to the achievement of overall objectives.

The problem was put by Brian Simon that 'if each child is unique, and each requires a specific pedagogical approach appropriate to him or her and to no other, the construction of an all-embracing pedagogy, or general principles of teaching, becomes an impossibility' (Simon, 1981, p. 141). For Simon, to start from the standpoint of individual differences is to start from the wrong position. In his view:

'To develop an effective pedagogy means starting from the opposite standpoint, from what children have in common as members of the human species; to establish the general principles of teaching and, in the light of these, to determine what modifications of practice are necessary to meet specific individual needs (ibid.)'.

This was posed slightly differently by Sarup (1983, p. 131) in the context of work by the Italian, Antonio Gramsci, who insisted on the need for authoritative teaching and the disciplined application by the learner to academic work. Gramsci's point was that 'the purpose of schools is to develop a critical consciousness through intellectual application' (Sarup, p. 139) an objective many, but not all, progressives would also endorse.

There are thus disagreements among 'progressives' on particular aspects of teaching and learning, including how authoritarian teaching should be, but most, including socialists, are united in their belief in the educability of all children and adults. All share a determination not to restrict them by forcing them into outworn categories, just as all reject the reductionist biologism which has dominated educational thinking for much of this century. The education of all who teach and lecture should be based on a genuine concern that education should promote cognitive growth for everyone at every age.

Doubts about the 'National' Curriculum

What the content of early-years learning should be is another matter about which debate has yet to take shape in any large-scale way. But experience and projects to date can point the way, once the universal right becomes a reality. The main objective is to avoid the heavy-hand of government directives and prescription along 'nationalist' lines. Early years learning must remain flexible to respond to the new demands placed upon it in a wide diversity of communities; the views of parents and teachers should be able to be heard on this matter in ways that have not happened before.

The same could also be said for the education of the 5-16 age range, where the views of those involved have been progressively sidelined while political voices at the top laid down the law about what shall be learned as well as how it shall be learned. This dictatorship of study has been disturbing to both conservative and progressive critics, especially where there is a commitment to libertarian principles or to democratic innovation. While progressives oppose it for restricting learning, many conservatives have long opposed the idea of a 'National' Curriculum on various grounds, including the argument that in a 'true' market system, each school's curriculum would be one of its main selling points.[20]

Thus the years 5-14 are still dominated by controversy over the National Curriculum, a concept that initially found favour with those who had always supported a common entitlement curriculum (and within each school a common curriculum) as the appropriate companion of a common education system. But the way it has been developed for some schools only (omitting private education, for example) and particularly the segregation of knowledge and skills into outdated subject divisions, excluding so many vital areas, makes it plain that the National Curriculum is not a common curriculum but rather a rigid, over-controlled and highly prescriptive exercise, whose ostensible objective, some assume, is to return the country to a mythical past when a Christian monocultural orthodoxy held sway.

This orthodoxy seems to be entirely negative and based on the need to dismantle the increasingly international perspective of education and turn it back to the past. Underneath, the National Curriculum is not about commonality at all; it is about various forms of nationalism and ossified subject teaching. For all these reasons it is fatally flawed and adherents have steadily dropped away.

There was also the initial problem of imposing incredible paper work loads on teachers and requiring timetables that were impossible to implement in schools. Teachers and parents naturally rebelled. When opposition to the changes reached crisis point in 1993, Ron Dearing's hastily convened Committee was given the task of making alterations that dealt with the two greatest problems: namely, the impossibly overburdened timetables schools were experiencing, and the sinister insistence on an array of national tests to accompany each key stage.

It was the tests that alerted everyone to the fact that the National Curriculum's second hidden purpose had always been to justify the reintroduction of '11-plus' testing. Now that universal tests are being published, and being used for selection no one is any longer left in doubt. Undermining comprehensive education has long been an objective of conservatives, as their spokespersons have made plain on many occasions from the 1960s through to the 1990s.

Replace the National Curriculum with an entitlement curriculum

By contrast, those who have supported comprehensive change have generally favoured an entitlement curriculum. In the 1980s and 1990s they have tried valiantly to find a way of using the National Curriculum to forward this development first spelled out by Her Majesty's Inspectorate (HMI) in the 1970s. For there is a strong case for an entitlement curriculum throughout the 5-16 age range—where 'areas' of knowledge are covered with schools left free to teach them in their own way. It is not, however, the 1904 grammar school curriculum written on the back of an envelope by the politician Kenneth Baker and his civil servants in 1987 without any genuine professional input from teachers, much less consultation with any of those likely to be affected, including parents, students and HMIs.

This failure to consult those working within, and using, the system, lies at the root of the National Curriculum and its ongoing difficulties, for had Baker done so he would have discovered how far education had moved on from his own school days. Simply drawing up a list of ten or eleven old-style 'subjects' and calling it a National Curriculum has become a travesty of considered curriculum planning and it has put genuine curriculum development on hold for years, leaving a National Curriculum that is in constant need of far-reaching modification, if not actual dismantling.

During the period of the Dearing Review, teachers were lulled into a false sense of 'ownership' by being afforded the (unusual) experience of having their views (and those of their professional associations) taken into consideration. But there seems to be little point in simply 'slimming-down' the requirements of the National Curriculum unless we are clear about just how prescriptive such a curriculum should be and whether its goals, hidden and open, are acceptable.

On to the common curriculum

More and more teachers and parents wish to move to a common curriculum (agreed by each school for all its pupils). This would be much more under the control of the individual school and those who teach and learn within it. It is far more compatible with the aims of comprehensive education and better able to be adapted to the huge variety of schools that exist. At 16-plus the aim would be a common core, a learning programme experienced by everyone in each school or college for a stated minority of their time, regardless of their main fields of study.

How then should a school decide what its students should be learning in common during the 5-16 period? Writing in 1993, Cary Bazalgette, Principle Education Officer, British Film Institute (BFI) Media and Education Research, pointed out that there are both good and bad ways of arriving at a worthwhile professional common curriculum for our schools:

> 'The bad way is to itemise minimal, testable skills and list study
> objects, within ring-fenced traditional subjects. The good way ...
> is to agree and summarise the essential principles for each area
> of a faculty-based curriculum which ... will enable and endorse
> purposeful teaching and learning across the full range of cultural
> experience' (Bazalgette, 1993, p. 15).

It is important that any Common Curriculum should not lay down the totality of a child's education. It must ensure a child's entitlements in terms of areas of experience, which can then be used as the basis of rational curriculum construction. It must also be the outcome of wide-ranging debate and enquiry, which should start with the views of teachers and parents—and pupils—within the schools. As Hillcole argued earlier, a national curriculum in a democratic society should be:

> 'neither the 'secret garden' of the professionals, as in the past, nor the present centrally imposed one. It should be based on a nationally agreed statement of entitlement arrived at through wide debate, but be flexible enough to be elaborated upon by educationalists, students, parents and community groups at a local level, to meet local needs. There would need to be a balance within the curriculum between the needs, aspirations and interests of the individual student and the needs of the community and the wider world' (Hillcole, 1991, p. 92).

We further emphasised that:

> 'To ensure that all students achieve their full potential, the curriculum—both formal and hidden—should actively discourage inequalities of access and outcome on the basis of class, 'race', sex, sexuality and disability. The curriculum should be secular in its orientation but should value and take account of the cultures, languages, skills and experiences that students bring with them.'
> (p. 93).

Thus over and above the way a secondary system is organised, we need attention to the experience of learning and teaching, to deal with the largely unacknowledged failure of our present system to retain the interest or commitment of so many young people. This is far more likely to occur if we recognise that the world in which they are being educated is one requiring an international understanding in which advanced technology will allow different cultures and traditions to speak for themselves. All attempts to turn the clock back to an aggressive Anglo-Christian centred perspective should be resisted.

In the 21st century, when parents and teachers and members of any community are making their views known about what is being studied in local schools and colleges, as a matter of course in a democratic society, we will marvel at the world of the 1980s and 1990s when the whole of Britain remained without real voice, waiting for politicians to decide these matters for them.

C. Today's testing: Ostensibly about assessment but really about 'ranking'

After a year of conflict between government and teachers over the issue of testing, the final report of the first Dearing Review (*The National Curriculum and its Assessment*, 1993) appeared to represent some sort of victory for professional opinion. But it failed to clarify the purposes of testing, the issue over which many teachers had carried out one of the most effective industrial campaigns since the second World War.

Most teachers understand that the school curriculum should not be determined by testing arrangements. Organisations like the National Union of Teachers (NUT), for example, have always been totally consistent in opposing the current tests at all stages on educational grounds. Assessment of pupils by tests may be necessary to diagnose and facilitate the progress of each individual, but current testing arrangements are clearly intended to 'rank' schools and teachers rather than to support pupils or help schools to improve their teaching (other than their 'teaching to the test').

There is growing hostility to all such ranking, but particularly deep and widespread hostility from parents and teachers to '11-plus' testing at the ages of 7, 11, and 14 used for the purpose of school 'league tables' and admissions rather than to give parents and teachers information about pupils' attainment levels (made clear in successive professional organisations' conferences from 1994 through 1996 and in opinion expressed by schools and colleges.)[21]

The present government will be tested by whether it can preserve the validity of the best assessment tests while rescuing the education system from the pernicious grip of league tables.

Standards are not raised by governments testing students competitively, or playing off school against school. They are raised by schools and colleges, teachers and learners, improving the work they do; and by giving those who teach and learn, and the institutions they use, the support and help they need. New government programmes are being planned to try to do this in literacy and numeracy and everyone hopes they will succeed. But how much change will be possible when so little else about the system these programmes are seeking to influence, is going to change?

14-18 Assessment needs radical reform

'11-plus' testing on the present league table principle should be ended as soon as possible and replaced by an arrangement that enables all schools and teachers to draw upon a national bank of attainment tests for various ages and areas of experience—and, if they wish, to take part in devising their own assessments. They could be used by schools individually at any time in the course of schooling. But it would be teachers and learners, schools and colleges that decided.

Giving teachers back their rights to play a full part in assessing the courses of learning they devise and teach, is another requirement to return testing to its true purpose, and their deserved autonomy to teachers. Assessment is there to enable learners to know where they are, and teachers to assess individual and group progress, as well as to diagnose strengths and weaknesses.

In time we could introduce for older students the pedagogic principle that all learners should have an understanding of, and, where possible, a share in defining, the type of assessment appropriate for whatever they are learning. Involvement in assessment is more likely than external testing to make students and teachers at all levels think about what they are learning and how they are learning it.

Every pupil and student should have a right to see the results of all testing or assessment that applies to them and to the class group and year group, and to relevant regional or national scores. All those in any institution, or with an interest in it, should be able to know the way its various age groups are assessed and what the outcomes have been in all the fields where assessment has been carried out. How information is reported more widely would be a matter schools and colleges could decide individually, together with their locally elected bodies.

Some might want to publish a few raw results, as they do now. But many more would want to publish results with the relevant facts relating to their schools' or their pupils' background. Some will want to publish 'value-added' tables, showing the way their school has (or has not) improved the entry scores of those they teach. But most would want to make clear the full range of courses the school or college offers, as well as the range of qualifications obtained and all the results that have been achieved within their walls, not just those few previously used. Nor would one score alone out of the many be used for 'ranking'. Since criteria for judging 'standards' varies so widely, it should be left to parents and communities and anyone else interested to do their own 'ranking' according to their own criteria. And to include criteria relating to social, cultural and sporting achievements.

The practice of lining everyone up on one 'academic' score alone from one exam alone, especially when it is a score only half the students in the UK currently attain, is a crude and wasteful practice that downgrades the talents of half the students in schools, including many with other types of intelligence, expressed in attainments and qualifications of differing kinds. Little wonder that the majority of schools believe league tables do not reflect their academic achievements fairly.

The testing we want to see would be designed to improve performance throughout the system, not to rank individual institutions or students. If any government or any local community wants to compare the progress of different groups, regions or ages in a thorough and scientific way, standard sample testing is always available to be used—as it is in most of the rest of the world. It is more informative, more cost-effective, less educationally disruptive, and many times more likely to raise standards than a system designed to promote the educationally 'rich' and shame the educationally 'poor', ensuring the two remain permanently divided.

14-18: Reducing the hurdles

Originally, the 'National' Curriculum applied to the last two years of compulsory education as to any earlier years. Whatever other faults it had, at least it was consistent in this respect. This consistency has now disappeared and Dearing's proposals for the ages of 14-16 abandon any commonality by endorsing separated paths on the lines of the 1950s: General Certificate of Secondary Education (GCSE) for the academic, new vocational courses for the 'non' academic (whatever that is), combined with permission for many students to drop essential areas of learning and to narrow their study considerably.

Changes for this age group will certainly be required but they will have to be undertaken in the context of the secondary system as a whole and with some understanding of the effect of developments on the 16-18 age group and beyond. Any changes must have the objective of encouraging the age group as a whole to stay in full-time education or training until 18 and of combining common curricular study with a method of choosing courses that gives each student a broad and balanced individual curriculum.

But changes in assessment are needed as well, particularly to the current examination system where a 16-plus examination acts as a hurdle that sorts out entrants suitable to continue in the divided system at the 16-18 stage: A levels for the academic and a bewildering variety of qualifications for others, relating to vocational education or to training competencies. Despite the many qualifications on offer (and some recent improvements in numbers staying on), the whole age group is by no means involved in either education or training after 16. Thousands leave every year as soon as it is possible for the simple reason that they do not find education rewarding. When one score in one examination sets the pace for all verdicts of success or failure (and anyone who does not achieve 5 good GCSEs is a 'failure' as the 'league table' culture proclaims), is it any wonder? Or any wonder that so many schools take less interest in young people thought unlikely to achieve this level by 16?

One of the main reasons why Britain has trailed badly behind most other countries in the matter of staying-on rates is that it is almost the only country with a major external examination held at 16, the same age as legal leaving is allowed (which some believe encourages many to leave once they have taken the exam). In addition, in a world where several advanced industrial nations have no external examinations at any stage, Britain is practically the only one which has two major national external examinations within two years of each other in the upper years of secondary schooling alone. It is hard to see how this system (which is also excessively costly) will achieve 100 per cent participation up to the age of 18, especially as improvement rates in recent years have been just as much due to the fact that there are no jobs as to some vague belief in the inherent benefits of attending for yet more education.

For a qualification that all can aim for, we need to redesign all courses and qualifications (from A level through the General National Vocational Qualification (GNVQ) and National Vocational Qualification (NVQ)) so that they will become parts of a single new secondary qualification. It would be a qualification that 100 per cent of the age group would be encouraged to take at 17 or 18. Meanwhile, the current GCSE would become an internally assessed stage at 16, or dropped altogether—with GCSE courses modularised within the same system as A levels and GNVQ. The numbers suggesting this reform continue to grow.

The 16-19 curriculum

We need to give a great deal of thought to the transition from a mainly common curriculum before 16 to one that is more diversified afterwards. Diversified should not mean divided. There must be no vocational versus academic pathways, and no package courses filled up with operative training, leaving no room for general education. All types of courses should be available for students to combine as suits their diverse needs and goals.

A clearly defined 'core' of study should be required of all those staying in education after 16, to include common study for all—possibly in the fields of English, science, mathematics, technology and a general humanities remit that could include the skills of critical enquiry. It might also encourage other language learning both by developing many students' mother tongues or local (e.g. Celtic) languages, as well as by visits abroad.

Exactly when and how the common element decreases and at what rate and whether it should start as early as 14 or wait until 16 is, again, a matter of debate. Sadly, this debate is not taking place nationally, since there is no proposal other than Dearing's so-called life skills to have any common element after 16 plus. In addition, there is no agreement about how soon and how much specialisation should be taking place, or whether every student should continue with a balanced learning programme, required to choose courses from both 'hand' and 'brain' fields, so that no-one emerges from schooling in the 21st century irrevocably allotted to one side or the other of the academic/vocational divide.

A complete redesign—not just a wider set of A levels

The second Dearing Review of post-16 qualifications (1996), though it earned critical acclaim for its balance and moderation, nevertheless leaves a lot of key questions unanswered. Above all, the fact that A levels remain untouched, and that it is left to schools and colleges to decide whether or not to offer the new certificates and diplomas, is a recipe for more, not less, confusion.

This could partly be met by redesigning the curriculum within a single new unified qualification where a wide range of course combinations could lead to a single national or regional certificate at the end of secondary education. This would be the objective of everyone entering the school system and would also be open to adults to take. They would be able to enrol in local schools for the purpose as well as in colleges.

The qualification would be defined by credits and these would be transferable and cumulative, a principle that should be extended beyond to education after 18. With the Open University having already pioneered such a system in Britain, it cannot be tagged as odd or unworkable. Indeed, it could turn out to be a prerequisite of high standards in a new century which would find the old externally examined single final examination, designed in the 19th century, the odd one out.

Within such a new structure, individual course work, together with collective practical learning projects of use to their participants and their communities, would be able to find a secure place. A wider variety of learning styles, along with a far greater range of student-and-teacher-chosen testing and examinations, would also be possible. Likewise, locally determined and individually negotiated learning programmes could be included and developed. All these are areas to which very little attention has been given, although there are several models which offer guidance (see Harber, 1995; Hatcher and Jones, 1996).

The objective is to balance the need for diversity, with the assurance that a common entitlement will be honoured. When a start has been made on implementing a new system, possibly locally-based curriculum forums might continue discussion on the way new developments (which none can foresee) might be accommodated. For example, some could be related to learning for, from and at paid work by Training Councils as proposed by the Trades Unions Congress (TUC).

Widespread discussion with all those likely to be affected is essential, not just when implementing a new system but also in developing it. This consultation must allow sufficient time to make sure plans are workable. We want no repeat of unworkable conservative changes (still sometimes referred to as 'reforms') implemented overnight, only to be dismantled almost immediately. It might be worth investigating the idea of a rolling development plan covering a decade or more.

Changes in assessment after 18, which will also be required as more and more students undertake life-long learning, will be much easier to develop once the log jam of 14-18 has been cleared.

D. The structure, funding and organisation of the system

5-16 structure

Along with the redesigning of the curriculum and qualifications should go new developments in the organisation of the learning system. There should be no repeat of the 1965 comprehensive change when the structure alone was changed (but not assessment nor the curriculum), nor of more recent changes where the curriculum gets changed while the structure steadily regresses, increasingly characterised by insupportable inequalities.

In devising educational developments in each area or region (impossible now in a centralised system imposing a market free-for-all), locally elected bodies must be given back powers to co-ordinate and consult and eventually decide (within national guidelines) what is acceptable to, and workable within, each local area or region.

The national guidelines should include an overhaul of the chaotic and inequitable admissions systems to schools and colleges, with backing for a system that is manifestly fair and equitable. Such a system should give clear legislative backing to ruling out selection on grounds of attainment. It would enable local and/or regional authorities to plan coherently for future development, secure in the knowledge that all state-funded institutions will have the same rights and the same consideration and be operating under the same equitable legal conditions in matters like admissions and funding. These changes are especially important if schools are going to be encouraged to become more diverse.

Post-16 structure

There should be an end to the encouragement of proliferation of small and uneconomic sixth forms which has continued for nearly twenty years, most recently fostered by the unrelenting pressure to get schools to 'opt out'. It has removed resources from the earlier years of education and not necessarily benefited students after 16. This is why there should be a start to the co-ordination of post-16 education, again involving all institutions in each area or region with students over this age.

No one institution can offer everything at 16-19, so institutions will need to plan co-operatively to cover 'all that is normally available for the age group' and make it available for everyone in every area—one of the key criteria of comprehensive education identified in the 1950s. It is time to end the wasteful contest between sixth forms and sixth form colleges and further education colleges for the 16 plus student—with its shocking failure to ensure equal choice for all, along with costly duplication, waste, and inefficiency, not to mention gaps in particular areas of provision in many areas of the country.

All institutions currently catering for post-16 students will need to be drawn together to provide for expansion in a common and co-operative exercise, and agreement reached on where new institutions or outposts of those already existing, should be sited. And agreement on how courses in each area could be shared, each institution having a balanced intake of students and offering a good balance of learning. There should be no division between academic and vocational study in the 16-19 years since policy should be to encourage a broad and balanced curriculum. In any case, the majority of students want to be free to choose a combination of study involving both.

Where possible, tertiary colleges, favoured so strongly by so many of all political complexions (and on course to be the standard new development until the middle of the 1980s) should be encouraged. They have stood the test of time. But where they are not possible, schools and further education colleges could pool their work, guided by decisions they make together as institutions serving a common area. Included in this work of integration should be the relevant courses at higher education institutions and all local training, wherever it is taking place. Arrangements for institutions to receive funding according to their provision and original rolls at the start of any year would be easily devised, leaving students themselves free to choose study from a range of sites or venues. Once co-operation has become the organising principle, solutions will fall into place far more easily.

Training is part of education

All young people in training up to 19 (with or without jobs) should be regarded as being in education. They should have the same rights as students on full-time college courses or in sixth forms or in the upper standards of secondary schools. All young people up to 18 should have the same status and rights within the education system. No one should be allowed to employ anyone under 18 without releasing them to education and training as part of their continuing part-time study for the national secondary qualification.

At the same time, all jobs should have a well-structured training component, available to those entering work from any age group. There is no job that should fail to carry with it a component of education and training—both general education for the benefit of the job holder, and specific training for the development of the work itself.

Learning from work should be linked to education at all stages, and trainees, including those being trained on employers' premises below the age of 19, would be overseen in the same way as students of comparable age within the education system. Over 18 they would be supported as adults in learning are supported, and attached to local publicly supported colleges or overseen by elected local bodies, with new powers and duties in respect of training courses in the workplace or in private agencies as well as inside the state-supported college. At present, the student in a sixth form has the oversight of governors, but the trainee under 18 has no such assistance or redress if required. Nor do many trainees over 18.

All trainees should have the right to join an appropriate trade union; and unions should have rights to explain their work to all who enter training. This would include the union's own education programmes, for in future many trades unions will wish to become equal partners with employers and educational institutions in overseeing or providing training and education to those at work. This is just one example of the way many different kinds of organisations and voluntary bodies will themselves be taking part in education and training in the future.

Increasingly, too, higher and further education colleges will form partnerships with each other, and with schools, as well as undertaking the early years of degree-level study in collaboration with local universities. Particular activities, for example running special programmes for school-age children or help in augmenting schools' provision in particular areas of learning (music, languages or sport) are the kind of developments that could be effected through joint provision, especially on weekends and in the holidays. Equally closely related is support for those who continue their education while at work, or at home, both as much part of the education system as those studying inside institutions. The system has to be organised and developed to support and encourage all these learners. Many interesting suggestions for extending the work of public education services in these ways can be found in the Kennedy Report on widening participation (FEFC, 1997).

New divisions on the horizon after 18?

Yet just as old divisions go, new ones seem to assert themselves, particularly as a result of the way the competitive market in education and training has been promoted by conservatives. Thus as the old 'binary' divide between polytechnics and universities beyond 18 has ended, with all having university status (save a forgotten college sector of HE), new divisions are being revealed. This is not just between Further Education and Higher Education but also between an 'ivy league' of top colleges and the rest. This last is moving into place informally. This has seen research increasingly concentrated in special centres, while new (and some not so new) universities are pressured into becoming teaching-only institutions, where skills courses, narrowly related to employment, will be concentrated, along with two-year degree programmes and franchised first-year degrees in local colleges.

At the top end of higher education in the 'ivy league' colleges, courses unrelated to any specific employment will remain, serving as a cultural apprenticeship for those destined already for higher management and top professional jobs—often jobs for life. Fees raised to full cost for such prestigious courses can be anticipated as colleges in the antique universities are tempted to privatise themselves out of the publicly supported system, raising their entry requirements rather than admitting more students or extending themselves to serve an ever wider range of adult students in any serious way.

Increased business sponsorship at all levels, further distorting the range of learning, can also be expected. The distinctive contributions of the former polytechnics will be lost just as the ideal of the comprehensive schools and local further education colleges is being compromised now by the privatisation and polarisation engendered by the 1988, 1994 and 1996 Education Acts.

Meanwhile, in the FE/HE sectors, many colleges that do not attain university status will merge or die—despite the new emphasis given to further education in statements made since 1992. FE college closures and mergers are always threatened as a result of competition for students in the new phoney 'marketplace', including off-the-wall voucher-for-everything proposals. Despite the relative increase in further education numbers, the funding position of further education remains more critical than ever. Yet this sector will be the lynch-pin of educational advance for the majority of adults in the 21st century. It is the sector that has always offered a second chance to those failed by their schooling, in close relation to training in and for work; it is the sector where future national funding and expansion should concentrate.

Increasing numbers are also being recruited in higher education, including more mature students. We welcome this development, despite the fact that accommodation, staffing and expenditure are not expanding to meet the needs of these students, thereby jeopardising current developments from the start. Expansion on the cheap should not be an option, and could well self-detonate, as, inevitably, students at all levels experience hardship, inadequate teaching and severely overstretched facilities—not to mention government attempts to restrict their freedoms through their meddling with student union rules, or to shackle their funding through draconian loan arrangements.

Post-18 learning: developing the comprehensive principle

Even with more funding, simply cramming more bodies into existing courses is not the answer to life-long learning. The whole nature and range of higher education needs to change. The change required is a development of post-18 institutions along the lines of the changes in secondary schools in the 20th century, in a comprehensive direction: institutions in each region working together to provide a full range of courses normally associated with education after 18, for those in their region as well as those outside it who can be attracted into use them.

In time, every region should have its higher education institutions providing the hub of a learning infrastructure, so that anyone living anywhere within it has access to this same full range. And in those few areas where this may not yet be possible, the new information technology should be used to assist, while in time many new venues for learning will be established: in homes, workplaces, and within the community.

As with secondary education, changes are also required in what is learned after 18. New degrees, for example, are required in subjects that have social and environmental relevance, while narrow business courses—and all economics courses—need to have long-neglected social input at every stage. More flexible transfer arrangements, term times, and course combinations are needed.

Dearing is already dated

A rational, planned, and long-term reorganisation of higher education, taking all these factors into account, is what we are suggesting, not the partial adjustment that the third Dearing *Review of Higher Education* suggests. For meaningful change to have taken place that will enable the majority of adults to continue learning throughout life, with a system in place for the year 2020 or even 2050, a much more ambitious long-range overhaul is required.

Whatever the size of local government, the planning of training and education after 18 in any area, including the universities, would have to be of a comprehensive nature and on a regional basis. Scotland and Wales already run most of their own institutions. The various regions of England could do so as well. Institutions would be given the largest measure of devolved control consistent with equality between them and their regionally elected bodies' duties in respect of them. And much of the money now going in grants from the centre should be passed to the regional governments to distribute between their institutions, including universities. National programmes and more funding in future would thus go as much to support courses within institutions as to the institutions themselves.

Within the various post-18 institutions, need would have to be determined in relation to a set of well-defined factors (as at school level). Unlike the present demented 'funding' methodology, this will be related to the requirements of size, special areas of expertise, research capacity, together with the region's social needs and the speed with which institutions like universities move to greatly enlarge their entry of local residents. Higher education must be encouraged to provide far more fully for the adult population locally if expansion within likely budgets is to be achieved. This 'comprehensive' commitment to the whole of the adult population, assuming all have an equal right to education during their lives, is what will radicalise the provision and funding of future learning within all institutions and organisations with adult learners whether they be universities, further education colleges, or voluntary programmes.

In time, there would be one sector only: the post 18 sector—with a variety of colleges, institutions, venues and organisations providing a learning infrastructure for a very diverse population from traditional degree level study to the development of local training initiatives for an area's services and manufacturing industries. These too relate to the way university and college education can be expanded within the expenditure likely to be available in the near future.

Part-time: the new norm

In order to accommodate a vast increase in adult learners, most post-18 education will have to be conceived in terms of the 'commuting' distances adults can travel to attend courses or undertake training or liaise with distance learning tutors. This does not preclude students choosing residential experience at a far distance, including exchanges abroad, but it would recognise that residential students as a proportion of the total post-18 population will probably decrease dramatically as the 21st century progresses—in part because future students will include such a large portion of mature students already resident in the area and unwilling or unable to leave it.

Another challenge FE and HE colleges will be required to adapt to is to enable all degree level work, or constituents of that work, to be undertaken part-time as well as full-time. This means adults can continue studying while also working or bringing up their children or continue their own education when their children leave home. The education system cannot remain forever modelled on some sort of finishing school for an exclusive group of accelerated young students straight from school, without any personal ties, who are shooting through in three years with the lucky ones on their way to lucrative employment for life. This sort of 'Dearing' student will not disappear but he or she will become ever less typical—especially when it is finally understood that 'higher' education is there for taking up at any stage in life. It does not have to be taken during those particular three years.

Rarer too will be full-time students supported with full-time financial assistance (whether grants or loans) at the universities, while those in hundreds of other colleges receive little or no financial support in respect of their learning. A catalyst to change will be to end the priority given in student maintenance to the 3-year full-time undergraduate course, shifting relatively more and more support and funding to those who are studying part-time. An important principle will be that the level at which anyone is studying is not the main factor that should condition the basic support individual students receive.

In a system of life-long education, most post-school students will not be teenagers and most will be studying part-time as part of normal working existence. The feasibility of introducing such a system that genuinely offers opportunities to all at reasonable cost depends in part on the revolution in educational methods that is coming from advances in information technology, partly on the way resources are redistributed, and partly on changes in the way learning will be organised.

Redesign and simplify the system for life-long learning

The traditional system consisted largely of a limited number of places in courses which were total packages of institutional attachment, timetable, teaching, resource, welfare, subsistence and examinations. We must now plan on replacing this by a system in which this package is disaggregated—with each part available separately. The governing principle will be completely open access to curriculum content, software, facilities, and assessment, together with an appropriate level of tutorial assistance and advice designed to help students succeed.

The evolution of life-long education, with the part-time adult learner at the heart of most institutions, represents an inevitable shift from the concept of university as an extension of boarding school, while the information revolution renders obsolete many of the traditional processes of university teaching and learning. By 2020 the achievement of first degree standard should be no more exceptional than four or five GCSEs are today. It will not require 3 years seclusion and it will not be inhibited by the assumption that only an academic much occupied with research and publication, is fit to assist.

From schooling onwards new developments will demand a greater measure of standardisation and a greater separation of teaching from examinations. Within ten years we can expect progress in establishing a system of credit accumulation and credit transfer. This will be followed by a growth in a small number of examining bodies in higher education that are independent of teaching institutions, enabling students to accumulate educational qualifications autonomously—in their own time and when they judge themselves to be ready to be assessed.

Help will be sought by students of the future from a wide range of experts, including technicians, librarians, and fellow students, where most students get considerable (and often unregistered) help already. The model that points the way to the future is not the 19th century university but the Open University as well as such independent study degrees as were pioneered by the former Polytechnic of East London and Lancaster University. The new-style learning will include many new variants on the themes of 'sandwich' and 'block release' education that have developed since 1950. The majority of educational interests cannot be pursued in ivory towers; mature students cannot ignore family commitments; study is not always enhanced by separation from the real world.

Disaggregation: Towards a better balance between research and teaching

Research and academic study for their own sake must retain their place, of course, but insofar as most students do not want to be full-time academics and researchers, it is not necessary that almost all their teachers are solely preoccupied with research priorities. Disinterested study and creative effort have to be supported but it is clearly inappropriate that a system of mass education should be dominated by those committed primarily to traditional research requirements, and that so large a proportion of university budgets should be committed to financing the private concerns of university teachers in ways that give these far higher importance than teaching capacity.

The disaggregation of research expenditure from teaching expenditure in higher education is both inevitable and desirable. This will free the researcher, but it will also give more students a greater choice of routes and learning methods, and a better quality of assistance, when institutions lose their cartel-like grip on examinations and the awarding of degrees and diplomas. It will also extend the work of further education institutions and schools if their own staffs have opportunities for research themselves. For if it is reasonable to say that teachers in universities should be intellectually and academically active and that this activity should be part of their job, it should also be true of all teachers in all sectors of education. What is important is that the cost of research in any institution is given separately from the costs of teaching—so that we are not misled by statistics showing it is so much more 'expensive' to each a mathematics course in a university than to teach the same course in a further education college.

At the same time as extending teaching methods, we should be redefining research to make it more inclusive and practitioner-based where appropriate. This means linking useful social and scientific research, artistic creation and technical invention—and scholarly investigation—to the individual and collective project work that we have suggested also needs to be fostered at all levels of learning.

Asserting the vital role of learning in all sorts of cultural and recreational areas, including sport and the arts, as well as generating democratic reconstruction, represents a reassertion of the service ideal of institutions like the polytechnics, putting it on a par with the university ideal of traditional humanism. It means teachers and learners at all levels will have academic freedom to pursue pure research on behalf of scientific and cultural advance. To accommodate these shifts we would need to formulate a clearer definition of the purpose and function of such scientific research, artistic creation and academic scholarship in relation to other types of intellectual activity, particularly those taking place outside the universities—not only in industry and business but just as important, in local communities and regions, even individual estates and neighbourhoods. This would be a salutary experience for many academics; after all, as Einstein said, 'If an expert can't tell a layman what he does in five minutes, then he is not an expert'.

Democratic goals and the limits of modular systems

The aim of our proposals is to ensure the multi-skilling of the majority and the empowering of their democratic participation in order to control not merely their personal choice of the commodities presented to them, but by generalising power to control the future direction of society and its relation to the world's economy and ecology. Thus these objectives should be kept in sight during all individual and collective programmes of study in school and college, so that each will include some element of independent study or scope for some original discovery, creation or research. With new forms of assessment and self-assessment based on their work, this is possible.

Investigation, experiment and debate by all students, and as many others as possible, are vital today when so many received ideas in the social and natural sciences are (or should be) open to question. In addition, new technology can be applied at every level of learning to facilitate routine memorisation and allow imagination free rein beyond the immediate necessity to earn a wage or the constraints of production for profit. Vocational space within education for seeding new ideas must be defended from constriction in programmes and over-directed learning methods and by making scientific research and artistic creation an integral part of the independent study of all students. This independent study should be designed across traditional 'subject' boundaries, and facilitated by the new modular systems of certification.

In a modular system, however, it is essential not to lose sight of the divisions between areas of knowledge as well as the interrelations between them. It is important to distinguish between defined areas of reality on the one hand, and, on the other, outdated and arbitrary academic 'subject' divisions. This is not to advocate a random 'pick-and-mix' approach. But we must realise that if everything is left to the market there is a loss of theoretical and general knowledge, replaced by specialised knowledge related only to single occupational tasks.

Philosophical discussion and guidance are required if the modular method is not to result in narrowing vocational goals at one end spiced with irrelevant educational consumerism at the other. Qualifications like the NVQ, for example, while employment-related, should not be employment-led. Educational interest must have the major influence. Such interests should be linked to Workplace Training Committees, as recommended by the TUC—with worker-based assessment in the NVQ involving workers in 'skills audits' rather than assessment by outside professionals. With all this work and study co-ordinated by further and higher education, validation would permit genuinely generalisable knowledge and skills between occupational sectors and workplaces.

A number of new national and international bodies will need to be established to determine curricula and conduct examinations. Closely associated with them, but independent from them, will be a number of national organisations charged with the development and publication of learning materials, including, not least, broadcast materials accessible through new and old information media.

Rationalise learning for life-long education

Most universities and colleges could be incorporated into new comprehensive networks by 2020, centred in the conurbations, open throughout the week and throughout the year. These will have branch facilities sited in smaller towns; in suburbs and in villages, possibly using local schools or other premises, as well as in homes, community venues and workplaces. Associated with these comprehensive clusters would be research institutes—either funded quite separately or supported by the institutions within the network.

Those who did not have the necessary qualifications to start on any course could either obtain them within the local schools or constituent colleges or avail themselves of access courses. Such courses in future should not be a matter of happenstance. All institutions catering for adults should be required to offer access courses themselves (or in co-operation with other local institutions), so that those not possessing the necessary combination or level of qualifying study can always undertake the study to qualify for entry. Such access provision should be required to meet local demand (and funded to do so by the regionally elected body), so that every route to all major fields of study and all major areas of work, professional and technical, remain open to all citizens, throughout life.

In this way the wishes of communities and students could influence provision just as much as disciplines of 'the market' as defined by employers. The job of the elected bodies overseeing expenditure would be to balance the two.

Subject hierarchies and the stratification of society

Just as we are no longer aiming to service *élites* who have been identified early on as good at specific subjects and give them leave to shoot up the system and monopolise resources, so too will we have to withdraw from a system that retains a hierarchy of subjects conditioning expenditure within the system. In its place we should be encouraging literacies and learning of many different kinds as part of the task of encouraging the multiple intelligences that people possess.

We should welcome the expansion of further and higher education, though not necessarily for the economic reasons commonly used to justify it, that it will enable Britain to 'catch up with foreign competitors' and so 'raise living standards'. These do not necessarily follow, for the partial moves towards a mass system already under way are primarily political responses to a new social situation. This involves the recomposition of the class structure that has been produced by the application of new technology in conditions of growing economic insecurity. It does not represent a rational response to our current economic crisis and cannot be justified by unfounded economic arguments.

To blame failures of the economy solely upon a lack of education and training, as governments have done since 1976, diverts attention from the real causes of Britain's declining position in competitive world markets which is clearly associated with underlying structural problems in the social and economic system—a system which all political parties continue to support uncritically. That is why an alternative education policy requires thinking about alternative approaches to the social and economic structure of our society as an integral part of thinking about long-term educational changes.

Short term changes without long-term reorganisation could even increase dissatisfaction, for what becomes apparent to most pupils during their secondary schooling is that they are caught in a system of stratification by examination and other means, sorting them for their future position in the labour market. This has been the prime source of disaffection with school for the majority of pupils in the past, especially those relegated to secondary modern schools in selective systems, or now, to 'comprehensives' in run down areas or surrounded by selective or GM schools—or, in increasingly streamed comprehensives, to the lower tracks.

'Cooling out' the majority at later and later stages can postpone disaffection inside the education system, but it cannot deal with it in society at large. The last thing we want is to forge a new system for adults after 18 that repeats these earlier faults and strives to set up a new hierarchy with new polarisation and new disaffection. Adults and their learning are far too diverse to take this chance; they require the comprehensive criterion of equal value for all learners and all learning, however different.

The struggle to benefit from information technology: Can democracy win it?

Nevertheless, the rhetoric of a learning society as it might exist requires us to think of the tremendous increase in learning required for a labour process based on the conscious involvement of all employees, together with a society of citizens active in their own working and democratic lives. For this to become reality, the culture of organisations would have to change. Changes cannot be imposed on the systems we have now, for individuals require confidence in their ability to undertake life-long learning or to adapt to new technologies and take on new work.

New technologies can enslave and manipulate especially in the hands of the multinationals now buying up the world's information super-highways for monopolistic profit making, but telecommunications and computing could also be used to reduce bureaucracy and to increase participation and democracy. There are many possibilities and local experiments should be started now to discover their limitations in relation to the self governance of as many areas of life as possible.

It is not only the mild reform of a voting system that needs attention, however inadequate the present system is perceived to be. Educational institutions can provide seedbeds for democracy, as the American educationist, John Dewey, proposed long ago, in order to improve the quality of political processes in a democratic society. He suggested that educational institutions and their students and staff should be organised as democratic groups, and that students should be taught to apply scientific method to problems of concern in their own communities, or to world problems with which they are concerned. Organising learning in democratic, problem-solving groups has always had potential, and could easily be revived.

Sharing knowledge means sharing power

Skills and competencies are not all that is required. It is new ways of working. That is why industrial democracy at work holds potential for those who usually exert very little control over the use of their labour power. Computer-integrated-manufacturing requiring fewer operatives and storing information communicated to all by all those involved in the operation—from engineers to managers to maintenance workers—potentially integrates objective decision making. This in turn could lead to the most logical form of organisation for optimum performance being co-operative and non-hierarchical.

New technology also extends opportunities for sharing information beyond production. In society generally, if knowledge is power, then power, like knowledge, needs to be shared. The basis for an informed democracy in which the majority exercise power instead of handing it over to a minority to rule over them, is just that: information and knowledge and (it is to be hoped) wisdom to use it for the survival of society and humanity.

Thus an integrated further, higher, and adult education and training system—operating end on from schooling—has a pivotal role to play in a real learning society. The first priority for any government seriously committed to real modernisation would be to re-establish the central purpose of education, science and the arts in society: as that which should stimulate thought and develop new knowledge and new skills to deal with a rapidly changing social and industrial reality.

This would be a real cultural revolution—not the partial 'skills' and 'enterprise' revolutions limited only to vocational preparation and individual competition, or simply learning for leisure, the limited visions usually suggested. Cultural production is essential not only for the increased education and training required for a labour process and a learning society consciously involving all citizens, but also to encourage the healthy maintenance of a world environment that the destructive production methods of market capitalism are threatening to lay waste.

The right to learn, the right to earn and the right to survive

To sum up, we return again to our first principle: work for all should be a basic right even if this is not the same as full-time employment in the old sense of 8 hours a day and five days a week, but rather the right to contribute to society by working, and in exchange for working, to receive a living wage. It should be a matter of progress that the long hours of work of yesterday are no longer necessary as a rule. Leisure can increase, as it would if work were genuinely shared. Thus the individual right to work must involve work-sharing to reduce hours worked not only in order to ensure that all have work to sustain themselves, but also to give those in work a chance to participate in increased learning at work as well as in cultural consumption out of work. This, in turn, will increase the market for cultural and recreational products and services.

Learning at all levels will be integral to such a real cultural revolution but will not be limited to formal education. It will include recreation, sport and many other cultural and self-directed activities, including the ecological and community activity urgently required in so many parts of our society. This could happen possibly through a Ministry of the Arts, Sports, Science, Education and Culture rather than the separation of all these activities.

But the right to socially useful work must be affirmed as one of the most basic human rights. In time it should be accompanied by the right to real training (all too often substituted for work) along with the right to education and recreation. In a real learning society training will no longer be differentiated from education and other cultural activities.

Human development: Society's purpose

Once education is no longer primarily about early selection for the employment hierarchy, we will be free to learn from work but never just in order to work. The demands of industry and service work have to be set in a wider framework of human, cultural and environmental development. To do so requires a far greater contribution of generalised knowledge within work-related education and training. This would include a curriculum that must lead to understanding the organisation of the economy as a whole as well as the relationships of power and possession that are involved in it.

Such a curriculum will insist equally upon making international connections, on understanding ' domestic' employment within the home as well as paid employment outside it.

Every learner and earner should be aware of the way social action relates to the larger political, economic and ecological system to which every community and individual belongs. Education should help citizens to run their own lives and institutions and communities more co-operatively and more peacefully. Each person and group should experience education as contributing to their own self-advancement, but at the same time our education should ensure that at least part of everyone's life activity is also designed to assist in securing the future of the planet we inherit—set in the context of a sustainable and equitable society.

Democracy is not possible unless there is a free debate about all the alternatives available for running our social and economic system. Fewer and fewer accept that there is only 'one way' to run an economy—either locally or world wide. Change will take place whatever we do. The only question is, will it be from a base of high general education throughout society or will it be controlled by ill-informed and media-manipulated precipitate action, as it has been in Britain in recent years, accompanied all too often by rigid reaction and increasing levels of exploitation?

All societies will be struggling with the same issues in the 21st century. We can prepare by being better armed with war machinery or more competitive international monopolies, both based on consuming ever more of the earth's resources in a society we are powerless to prevent from polarising and requiring ever growing expenditure on policing to oversee the unoccupied, uneducated, and ill-treated groups that such an approach creates.

Or we can wipe out poverty and the 'underclass' altogether. We can decide to approach the future by consciously putting our investment into a massive drive to encourage participation from everyone at every stage in life through training and education that will increase productive, social, cultural and environmental development in ways we have not yet begun to contemplate.

REFERENCES

Ainley, P. (1994) *Degrees of Differences: Higher Education in the 1990s*, London: Lawrence and Wishart.

Ainley, P. and Bailey, B. (1997), *The Business of Learning: Staff and Student Experiences of Further Education*, London, Cassell.

Bazalgette, C. (1993) 'From cultural cleansing to a common curriculum', *The English and Media Magazine*, 28, Summer, pp.12-15.

Benn, C. and Chitty, C., (1996) *Thirty Years On: Is Comprehensive Education Alive and Well or Struggling to Survive?*, London, David Fulton.

Benn, C., (1990) 'The public price of private education and privatisation', *Forum*, 32 (3) pp. 68-73 (refs. p. 93).

Blackman, S. J. (1996), 'Has drug culture become an inevitable part of youth culture? A critical assessment of drug education', *Educational Review*, 48, (2) pp. 131-142.

Burt, C. (1950) 'Testing intelligence', *The Listener*, 16 November.

Brehony, K. (1992), 'What's left of progressive primary education' in A. Rattansi and D. Reeder, *Rethinking Radical Education: Essays in Honour of Brian Simon*, London, Lawrence and Wishart.

Cole, M. and Hill, D. (1995) 'Games of despair and rhetorics of resistance': Postmodernism, education and reaction' *British Journal of Sociology of Education*, 16 (2) pp.165-182.

Cole, M. (1997), ' Equality and primary education: What are the conceptual issues?', in Cole, M., Hill, D. and Shan, S. *Promoting Equality in Primary Schools*, London, Cassell.

Cole, M., Hill, D. and Shan, S. (eds) (1997) *Promoting Equality in Primary Schools*, London, Cassell.

Commission for Social Justice, (1994) *Social Justice: Strategies for National Renewal*. The Report of the Commission on Social Justice chaired by Sir Gordon Borrie, London, Vintage Books.

CBI (Confederation of British Industry) (1989) *Towards a Skills Revolution*.

CBI (1994) *Training: The Business Case*.

Crombie White, R., Pring, R., and Brockington, D. (1995) *14-19 Education and Training: Implementing a Unified System of Learning*, London, The Royal Society of Arts.

Epstein, D. (1993), *Changing Classroom Cultures: Anti-racism, Politics and Schools*, Stoke-on-Trent, Trentham Books.

Furlong, J. (1993) 'Why wear blinkers?', *Times Educational Supplement*, 29 January.

FEFC (Further Education Funding Council) (1997) *Learning Works: Widening Participation in Further Education*. Report of a working committee on widening participation, chair: Helena Kennedy, Q.C.

General Household Survey (1995) *Living in Britain*, London, HMSO.

Green, A. (1994) 'Post-modernism and state education', *Journal of Education Policy*, 9 (1) pp. 67-83.

Harber, C., (ed.) (1995), *Developing Democratic Education*, Ticknell, Education Now Books.

Hatcher, R. and Jones, K. (eds) (1996), *Education After the Conservatives: Response to the New Agenda of Reform*, Stoke-on-Trent, Trentham books.

Hill, D. and Rikowski, G. (1997) 'Between postmodernism and nowhere: the predicament of the postmodernist', *British Journal of Education Studies*, 45 (2) pp. 187-200.

Hill, D. and Cole, M. (eds) (1998) *Promoting Equality in Secondary Schools*, London, Cassell.

Hillcole Group Papers, all London, The Tufnell Press:

(1991) *Changing the Future: Redprint for Education*.

(1991) *What's Left in Teacher Education* (Hill, D.).

(1993 a) *Markets, Morality and Equality in Education* (Ball, S.).

(1993 b) *Whose Teachers: A Radical Manifesto*.

(1993 c) *Falling Apart*.

IPPR (Institute for Public Policy Research) (1990) *A British Baccalaureate: Ending the Division between Education and Training*, London.

IPPR (Institute for Public Policy Research) (1993) *A Different Version: An Alternative White Paper*, London.

Joseph Rowntree Foundation (1997) *The Changing Distribution of the Social Wage*.

Labour Party, (1976) *16-19 Education*.

Labour Party, (1982) *Learning for Life*.

Labour Party, (1994) *Opening Doors to a Learning Society*.

Mortimore, P. (1997), 'Personally speaking', *Education Plus, Independent*, 27/03/97.

NCE (National Commission on Education) (1993) *Learning to Succeed: A Radical Look at Education Today and a Strategy for the Future*, London, Heinemann.

Paine, T. (1776) *Common Sense*, (1993 edition) Everyman, London, J M Dent.

Pring, R. (1983) *Privatisation in Education*, London, RICE (Right to a Comprehensive Education).

Plowden Report (1967), *Children and their Primary Schools*, London, HMSO.

Sarup, M. (1983) *Marxism, Structuralism, Education*, London, Falmer Press.

Schweinhart, L. J., Barnes, H. V. and Weikart, D. P. (with S. Barnett and A. S. Epstein) (1993) *Significant Benefits: The High Scope Perry Preschool Study Through Age 27*, Ypsilante, Michigan, High/Scope Press.

Simon, B. (1981) 'Why no pedagogy in England?', in Simon, B. and Taylor, W. (eds) *Education in the Eighties: The Central Issues*, London, Batsford, pp. 124-45.

Simon, B. (1996) 'IQ redivivus, or the return of selection', *Forum*, 38 (1) Spring, pp. 4-7.

Troyna, B. and Sikes, P. (1989), 'Putting the Why back into teacher education' *Forum*, 32 (1) pp. 25-28.

UN (1996) *Human Development Report.*

Watkins, P. (1993), 'The National Curriculum: an agenda for the nineties' in Chitty, C. and Simon, B. (Eds), *Education Answers Back: Critical Responses to Government Policy*, London, Lawrence and Wishart, pp. 70-84.

Walford, G (1990), *Privatisation and Privilege in Education*, London, Routledge.

NOTES

1 United Nations, *Human Development Report*, 1996

2 The Black Papers were a series of populist publications by conservative politicians, academics and journalists which supported academic selection and opposed comprehensive education. The first one was published in 1969 and the last in 1977.

3 See Pring, R. (1983) *Privatisation in Education*; Walford, G., (1990), *Privatisation and Privilege in Education*, p. 76; Benn, C., (1990) 'The public price of private education', *Forum*, 32 (3), pp 68-73.

4 ICM national poll, published *Guardian*, 7, 1996.

5 For example: Labour Party, *16-19 Education*, (1976) and *Learning for Life*, (1982).

6 *Living in Britain*, (1995), General Household Survey, Table 4.4. The percentage for women was 38 per cent, as more of the jobs women do (like supermarket checking out) is not classified as manual work. Classifications are based on jobs held by all persons aged 16 and over (or if unemployed, last held).

7 Elaine Kamarck, senior White House Policy Advisor, quoted in 'Education leads next term agenda', by Martin Walker, *Guardian*, November 2, 1996.

8 Institute for Public Policy Research (IPPR) (1990) *A British Baccalaureate: Ending the Division between Education and Training*; and IPPR (1993) *A Different Version: An Alternative White Paper*, Crombie White, R., Pring, R., and Brockington, D. (1995) *14-19 Education and Training: Implementing a Unified System of Learning*

9 See, for example, the speeches of government ministers in the House of Commons during the week of June 1 to June 5, 1997.

10 For a critical evaluation of post-modernism, including its supposed left-wing variants, see Green, (1994), Cole and Hill (1995) and Hill and Rikowski, (1997).

11 See, for example, two studies (one from the Harvard University School of Public Health and the other from the California Department of Health Services) both showing that in areas where the gap between rich and poor was wide, the health of the entire society was worse than in areas where the economic gap had narrowed. A summary of these studies was printed in the *British Medical Journal*, April 20, 1996. See also *The Changing Distribution of the Social Wage*, 1997, The Joseph Rowntree Foundation

12 See Cole (1997) for a detailed discussion of these conceptual issues and their relationship to primary, secondary and higher education respectively. See also Hill and Cole (1998).

13 House of Commons, Select Committee on Grant Maintained Schools, 1993, p.9

14 Audit Commission (1996) *Trading Places*.
15 Edgar Faure, French socialist, was one of the first to spell out the idea of '*education permanente*'.
16 See Reports, Youthaid, 1996 and 1997
17 Reported in 'The US Experience' by Gary Younge and John Carvel, *Guardian Education*, 22 April, 1997. See also Schweinhart *et al*. (1993) for the effects of nursery school attendance on African-Americans brought up in poverty.
18 *Changing the Future: Redprint For Education* (1991), *What's Left in Teacher Education?* (1991) and *Whose Teachers? A Radical Manifesto* (1993), Hillcole Group, London, the Tufnell Press
19 See Ainley, P. and Bailey, B., (1997).
20 For example, Keith Joseph, Angela Rumbold, Stuart Sexton, and Anthony O'Hear.
21 See David Hart, National Association of Headteachers (NAHT), *Times Educational Supplement*, 10 June, 1994; and reports of NUT April Conference, 1996, where a large number of teachers indicated support for a boycott of tests at 11 if plans went ahead. See also school and college opinion on league tables in Benn and Chitty, (1996).

GLOSSARY OF ACRONYMS

BFI	British Film Institute
CBI	Confederation of British Industry
FE	Further Education
FEFC	Further Education Funding Council
GCSE	General Certificate of Secondary Education
GM	Grant Maintained
GNVQ	General National Vocational Qualification
HE	Higher Education
HEFCE	Higher Education Funding Council for England
HMI	Her Majesty's Inspectorate
IPPR	Institute of Public Policy Research
ITE	Initial Teacher Education
LEC	Local Enterprise Council
NAHT	National Association of Head Teachers
NVQ	National Vocational Qualification
NUT	National Union of Teachers
NVQ	National Vocational Qualification
OFSTED	Office for Standards in Education
TES	Times Educational Supplement
TEC	Training and Enterprise Council
TTA	Teacher Training Agency
TUC	Trades Union Congress

Hillcole Publications

Changing the future: Redprint for Education
The Hillcole Group   edited by Clyde Chitty
Even Adam Smith said that education was too important to leave to the whim of the market place, and we must reassert the social principles on which education should be based, for the good of the individual and society. The Hillcole Group have laid down a challenge to all political parties, and revitalised the 'Education Debate' with a fresh vision of the future for education.
  210 x 150 mm 199pp   1991
  ISBN 1 872767 25 7   Paperback   £8.95

Equal Opportunities in the new ERA
Ann Marie Davies, Janet Holland & Rehana Minhas
The authors examine the implications of the 1990 Education Reform Act and the National Curriculum for equal opportunities in relation to gender, race and class.
  210 x 150 mm 52 pp   Second Edition   1992
  ISBN 1 872767 30 3   Paperback   £3.95

Something Old, Something New, Something Borrowed, Something Blue: Schooling, Teacher Education and the Radical Right in Britain and the USA
Dave Hill
Dave Hill examines Radical Right attacks on liberal-democratic and social-egalitarian models of schooling and teacher education in Britain and the USA.
  210 x 150 mm 37 pp   1990
  ISBN 1 872767 05 2   Paperback   £3.95

Training Turns to Enterprise: Vocational Education in the Market Place
Pat Ainley
Pat Ainley reviews the phases of education policy since the war and describes the reviews of vocational qualifications seeing in 'access' and modularisation the future direction of many education reforms.
  210 x 150 mm 28pp   1990
  ISBN 1 872767 10 9   Paperback   £3.95

Markets, Morality and Equality in Education
Stephen Ball
Stephen Ball explores the political and ideological antecedents of the education
market established by the 1990 Education Reform Act.
210 x 150 mm 22 pp   1990
ISBN 1 872767 15 X   Paperback   £3.95

**What's left in teacher education: Teacher education, the radical left and
policy proposals**
Dave Hill
Hill makes a series of challenging proposals for a Labour Government to enact.
He promotes the concept of the teacher as a critical reflective practitioner.
210 x 150 mm 59pp   1991
ISBN 1 872767 20 6   Paperback   £3.95

Falling apart: The coming crisis of Conservative education
The Hillcole Group
We argue in this pamphlet that the 'triumphalism' of educational conservatism
is hollow. Far from resolving the problems of education in England and Wales,
it is making them worse. Falling apart shows how the former Conservative
policy has creatied unmanageable organisational problems It is essential
reading for all who are committed to positive change.
210 x 150 mm 30pp   1992
ISBN 1 872767 35 4   Paperback   £3.95

Whose Teachers? — A radical manifesto
Hillcole Group
Teacher education in the 1990s is under pressure. The Hillcole Group presents
alternative proposals offering a democratic vision of teacher education which
is critical in the project of developing professional teachers for children and
the future.
210 x 150 mm 30pp 1993
ISBN 1 872767 40 0 Paperback   £3.00